LISTENING TO GOD

Colin Dye

Sovereign World

Sovereign World Ltd
PO Box 777
Tonbridge
Kent TN11 0ZS
England

Scriptural quotations are from the New King James Version, Thomas Nelson Inc., 1991.

ISBN 1 85240 208 3

This Sovereign World book is distributed in North America by Renew Books, a ministry of Gospel Light, Ventura, California, USA. For a free catalog of resources from Renew Books/Gospel Light, please contact your Christian supplier or call 1-800-4-GOSPEL.

Typeset by CRB Associates, Reepham, Norfolk
Printed in England by Clays Ltd, St Ives plc.

FOREWORD

The material in this *Sword of the Spirit* series has been developed over the past ten years at Kensington Temple in London as we have sought to train leaders for the hundreds of churches and groups we have established. Much of the material was initially prepared for the students who attend the International Bible Institute of London – which is based at our church.

Over the years, other churches and colleges have asked if they may use some of our material to help them establish training courses for leaders in their towns and countries. This series has been put together partly to meet this growing need, as churches everywhere seek to train large numbers of new leaders to serve the growth that God is giving.

The material has been constantly refined – by myself, by the students as they have responded, by my many associate pastors, and by the staff at the Bible Institute. In particular, my colleague Timothy Pain has been responsible for sharpening, developing and shaping my different courses and notes into this coherent series.

I hope that many people will use this series in association with our developing Satellite Bible School, but I also pray that churches around the world will use the books to train leaders.

We live at a time when increasing numbers of new churches are being started, and I am sure that we will see even more startling growth in the next few decades. It is vital that we re-examine the way we train and release leaders so that these new churches have the best possible biblical foundation. This series is our contribution to equipping tomorrow's leaders with the eternal truths that they need.

Colin Dye

CONTENTS

INTRODUCTION

Most church services seem to be filled with human speaking and human singing. The people appear to gather together to speak to God in prayer and thanksgiving, to worship him with hymns and spiritual songs, to speak about him in praise, and to listen to human preachers. Listening to *God* usually has a lower priority than speaking to God and singing about God.

There are some obvious reasons for this: for example, most believers really enjoy singing; they find it relatively easy to pray; and, from childhood, they have been well used to listening to people teach. In contrast, men and women today are increasingly uncomfortable with any form of silence, and they find the idea of actually listening to God rather strange.

Many congregations would be bewildered if their leaders announced that they were going to spend the next twenty minutes listening to God – the people simply wouldn't know what to do.

On the other hand, in the past decade, there has been a considerable increase in the numbers of Christian people claiming to hear God speak to them personally. The phrase, 'God has told me', must surely now be one of the most commonly heard expressions in many contemporary churches.

Yet some of the believers who make this claim find it difficult to explain how they have heard God speaking to them, and they have not been taught how to deal with the words that they have heard.

Listening to Almighty God must be fundamental to the life of faith and to every form of spiritual service. If we do not receive God's direction we cannot obey him; if we do not know how to recognise his voice, we can be led astray; if we do not know how to test revelation, we can act foolishly; and if we rarely consciously listen to God, our relationship with him is bound to be distant and superficial.

This is a book for believers who are willing to set aside their own preconceived ideas about listening to God, and are eager to study God's Word to discover God's revelation about this matter. We need to find out what the Scriptures teach about the way God communicates with his people, and – especially – what the Bible reveals about the way we should recognise and handle God's words.

Please make sure that you read each scriptural reference – and tick the margin reference boxes as you go along to show that you have. Answer every question and think through each point as it is made. Before moving on to a new section, think carefully about the implications of what you have studied. Please allow God to speak to you about your relationship with the Father as you study his word.

At the end of the book, there is some activity material and questions. Please make sure that you study Parts 1–9 before beginning to work through the activities, as this will ensure that you have an overview of the biblical teaching about prophetic listening before you try to apply the details of any one area. These questions will help you to grasp and apply the scriptural material that you have studied.

You will also be able to use the activity pages when you teach the material to small groups. Please feel free to photocopy these pages and distribute them to any group you are leading. Although you should work through all the questions when you are studying on your own, please don't expect a small group to cover all the material. Instead, prayerfully select those parts that you think are most relevant for your group. This means that, at some meetings you might use all the material whilst at others you might use only a small part.

By the time you finish this book, it is my prayer that you will have a better understanding of God's purpose in speaking, the process by which he speaks, and the scriptural principles involved in dealing with revelation. In particular, I pray that you will know his holy voice, will be developing a hearing heart, and will be ready to act on his words.

Colin Dye

PART ONE

prophetic listening

Every book in this *Sword of the Spirit* School of Ministry underlines the importance of listening to the living God.

For example, in *Knowing the Father*, *Knowing the Son* and *Knowing the Spirit*, we note that God is continually calling us into a deeper, more intimate, personal relationship with him – into a face-to face partnership which is characterised by mutual faith, love, commitment and communication.

He listens to us and we listen to him; he speaks to us and we speak to him; he gives himself to us and we give ourselves to him. If we do not keep on listening to God, we may be able to know the triune God *propositionally*, but we will never know the Father, the Son and the Spirit *personally* and *relationally*.

In *Living Faith*, we examine the vital link between our hearing of God's Word and the coming of God's faith. His living faith is planted in us when we listen to his Word and receive it deep into our spirits. As we keep on listening to God's Word – and as we go on believing, confessing and acting upon it – so the living faith of God becomes our own faith and develops towards maturity.

If we do not keep on listening to God, if we are not continually alert to his will and his Word, if we are not always in tune with his Spirit, we will not be able to live the life of faith to which we have been called.

In *Ministry in the Spirit*, we recognise that effective Christian service depends on believers listening to God to receive personal instructions and direction. Whenever we speak or act without having first heard his Word, we minister presumptuously: we develop *our* ministry rather than *his* ministry; we minister in the flesh rather than in the Spirit.

In *The Rule of God*, we see that the coming of God's kingdom in-and-with Christ means that the era of *legalistic obedience* to the Old Testament rules and regulations – including the Ten Commandments – has ended.

The advent of the kingdom of God is the coming, in-and-through Christ, of the personal rule of the Father: his redeemed children are called to a life of *gospel obedience* – which is a personal, divinely-enabled obedience to God's particular will in every circumstance and situation.

Before the coming of Christ, it was possible to know God's legal requirements by knowing the law of Moses. Since Christ, it has only been possible to know God's personal and particular rule by listening attentively to God, in the Spirit, to hear his will and his Word.

When, today, a church or individual believer neglects to listen to God, it is almost inevitable that they will drift into either licentiousness or legalism.

THE LISTENING PROCESS

One of the enemy's most basic ploys is to deceive believers into thinking that many of the most important parts of the Christian life are specific events rather than continuous processes.

The great truth that Christ's atoning death was *once-and-for-all* does not mean that each aspect of our faith is a similar 'one-off' event. For example, we note in *Salvation by Grace* that conversion is a process; we focus in *Living Faith* on the faith process; and we establish in *Knowing the Spirit* and *Ministry in the Spirit* that the giving of spiritual grace-gifts is a continuing equipping.

It is the same with listening to God. The devil attempts to deceive believers by suggesting a variety of lies – many of which are based on the idea that listening to God is an occasional action rather than a life-long activity.

The devil suggests, for example, that, if God has a message, he is quite capable of announcing it so loudly and clearly that it will break into our consciousness whatever we are doing. The demonic implication is that we do not need to listen to God because he will always make us hear him when he has something to say.

And the devil urges us to think that God is too busy, or too reluctant, or too holy to speak to us – and that we need to beg God to speak to us. He suggests that, if we ask God for long enough, he might – just once-in-a-while – deign to speak to us. He infers that God speaks to us only rarely, and that, therefore, listening is an occasional event rather than a unceasing activity. His diabolical aim is to prevent us from listening by persuading us to plead, unnecessarily, with God to speak.

This book often refers to *prophetic listening*. This does not mean that there are several different forms of listening, of which 'prophetic' listening is but one. Rather, the phrase 'prophetic listening' is merely a simple way of stressing that listening to God is a process and that it is also part of the wider prophetic process.

For example, listening to God is:

- *active not passive* – we do not listen to God like we listen to a piece of music – to be entertained; instead, we listen to him like a trainee pilot listens to his instructor – to be directed.

- *relational not functional* – we do not listen to God like we listen to a useful but anonymous help-line operator; rather, we listen to him like children listen to their parents.

- *continuous not occasional* – we do not listen to God like we listen to the radio, as-and-when we choose; instead, we listen to him continuously: we *listen to* God, we do not *listen out for* God.

- *rooted in the prophetic* – we listen to God like the prophets of old, in an intimate, anointed, servant relationship, ready to act on God's words.

Prophetic listening

The English words 'prophet', 'prophecy', 'prophesy' and 'prophetic' are derived from the Greek words *pro*, 'forth', and *phemi*, 'to speak'. They signify the 'speaking forth' of the mind and counsel of God.

The phrase 'prophetic listening' not only points to the place of listening in the prophetic process, it also underlines the fact that we are listening to the forth-speaking of the mind and counsel *of God*.

Prophetic listening is not a general, physical listening to the sounds that we can hear; it is a spiritual concentration, by faith, on the personal mind and counsel, on the revealed Word and will, of God. Although this book seeks to offer some practical guidance and biblical principles about the way we listen to God, the focus throughout is on God speaking – on the way he communicates his holy Word and will.

This means that prophetic listening is not a listening to silence, nor is it even a waiting in silence for God to speak; instead, it is an active spiritual listening to the God who is always communicating.

This *Sword of the Spirit* series constantly emphasises the prophetic calling of God's people, and stresses the importance of building faith and doctrine on an accurate understanding of the Old Testament.

Throughout the series, we learn that we should depend completely on the anointing of the Spirit and live in genuine partnership with the Holy Spirit; and we often note that the Old Testament prophets are fundamental to our understanding of faith and ministry.

In this book, we look even more deeply at the Old Testament and early church prophets – to learn from them about listening to God, and to see how our 'prophetic' listening should be applied in the church today. We consider the prophets in Parts Five and Six, and the prophetic application of our listening in Parts Seven to Nine.

APPRECIATING THE LISTENING PROCESS

In Parts Two to Nine, we study different aspects of the prophetic listening process. We consider the God who speaks, the ways that he speaks, and his purpose in speaking; we look at how the Old

Testament prophets listened to God, and see what they did with the revelation they received; we think about Jesus' prophetic ministry and his listening example; and we examine the biblical teaching about the ways that we should listen prophetically today and should handle revelation in the church.

Although each chapter focuses on a different aspect of the 'God speaking/ believers listening' process, there are some general 'over-all' principles that we should remember at every point in the process.

1.   Recognise that the living God is speaking

A sense of wonder will begin to shape and colour our thinking about prophetic listening when we start to appreciate our privilege at personally listening to Almighty God, to the Creator of heaven and earth, to humanity's great and gracious Redeemer.

The living God who speaks his mind and counsel to us is the same mighty God who made humanity in his image and dealt in grace with the Patriarchs. He is the God who parted the Red Sea, provided the Law, and protected his people in the wilderness; who smote Jericho, Goliath and Sennacherib; who sent fire to Carmel and shut the lions' mouths; who came in the flesh, sacrificed his Son, raised him from the dead and poured his Spirit onto the church.

This is the great God who speaks today to us – personally, privately, specifically, lovingly, graciously and continuously. We must take care, however, that our confidence in his will and willingness to speak does not lapse into presumption, over-familiarity and complacency.

One essential foundation of all prophetic listening is a deep sense of genuine awe at the thought of the living, loving God actually communicating with us. We simply must recognise, realise and remember *who* it is to whom we are listening.

2.   Realise that our listening ministers to God

Because it is God who calls us to listen to him, our listening not only builds, comforts, equips and guides us ourselves – it also ministers to God himself. Acts 13:2, for example, reports that the prophets and teachers at Antioch 'ministered to the Lord' as they listened to the Holy Spirit speak to them.

Acts 13:2

Many believers do not appreciate that their listening ministers to God – perhaps because they concentrate too much on what they can receive for themselves in the listening process. We must take care that we do not listen for self-centred purposes.

Prophetic listening is *relational* rather than functional, and God calls us to listen to him to deepen our relationship with him. This means that our prophetic listening ministers to him as much as it ministers to us. When we grasp this point, it should act as a spur to our listening.

3.   Remember the primary purpose of revelation

In Part Three, we learn that God speaks essentially to reveal himself to us. His revelation is always self-revelation. He speaks to us, *firstly*, so that we may know him better, and only *secondarily* so that we may know what to do or say in a particular situation.

When we start to consider biblical principles about handling prophetic revelation, and try to focus on the detail of what God is saying, we must not forget the larger revelatory picture.

Whenever we consider any aspect of God's forth-speaking and our prophetic listening, we must remind ourselves that the main thrust of the speaking/listening process is always that we may know him more intimately and accurately.

4.   Respond with obedience

It is pointless to listen to God without being willing to obey him and being ready to act on his Word.

In *Living Faith*, we see that the faith process involves hearing, believing, confessing and acting on God's Word. Faith is not biblical faith until every part of the faith process is in place. The seed of God's living faith will not mature in us if do not nurture it by obeying, confessing and acting on his Word.

It is the same in the listening process. It profits us nothing to listen to God and not demonstrate our belief by obeying and acting on his Word. In this book, by considering 'listening to God' within the wider prophetic process, we underline the truth that all the revelations we receive must be acted upon: we examine this in Parts Seven to Nine.

5.   Understand the process by which God speaks

The phrase 'listening to God' presupposes that God speaks. But, as God is a spiritual being, he does not *normally* speak audibly with a physical voice that we hear with our literal ears. Instead, he *usually* speaks in a non-physical way that we hear in our spirits by faith.

This book concentrates on the way that God communicates, because a biblical understanding of the divine revelatory process is essential for the avoidance of error, deception and manipulation.

We can begin to recognise God's voice only when we know how he speaks, but we are vulnerable to all sorts of false claims and ungodly voices when we are ignorant of the prophetic process.

6.   Develop a hearing heart

We have stressed that listening to God is a continuous process: we can express this in a different way by saying that we should develop a 'listening lifestyle' or a 'hearing heart' – for listening to God is fundamental to the believer's life of faith.

1 Kings 3:4–14 describes how God spoke to Solomon in a dream and offered him anything he asked. 1 Kings 3:9 reports that the new king asked for an 'understanding heart' so that he could 'discern between good and evil'.

1 Kings 3:4–14

Although the Hebrew word *bin* can be translated as 'understanding' or 'discerning', it points to a continuous receiving or hearing of God's understanding rather than to a once-and-for-all gift of wisdom. This means that Solomon was asking for *a hearing heart* rather than for encyclopaedic knowledge or a miraculous store of wisdom. This is why God was so pleased with Solomon's request.

In John 14:13, Jesus speaks to us in much the same way that God spoke to Solomon, promising us whatever we ask in his name. Surely no request is more in keeping with Jesus' words in John 14–16 than a plea for a 'hearing heart'.

John 14:13

As we move on to examine different aspects of the biblical teaching about God's forth-speaking and our prophetic listening, we will do well to ask God to give us a hearing heart – and we should then go on to do all that we can to develop this holy attitude in our lives.

PART TWO

the communicating god

It should be obvious that people who want to listen to God need to know who he is, what he is like, and how he communicates today. If we do not know him, we will not know how to listen to him.

For example, some people think that God is a material object like an idol – so they approach that object in their attempt to listen to him.

Others think that God is associated with natural features like the sun and the moon, trees and rocks, rivers and streams – so they draw close to these features to try to hear his voice.

And many people think that God is just an impersonal, invisible force who merely keeps the universe ticking over – they, therefore, do not even bother to try to hear him speak.

Of course, as Psalm 115:2–7 so dismissively points out, these pagan gods cannot even 'mutter through their throats'. In contrast, the living God of the Bible communicates clearly with the world that he has made through divine 'revelation'. From Genesis 3:1 to Revelation 22:17, on almost every page, the Bible describes God as speaking. In fact, the expression, 'says the Lord' is the commonest phrase in the Bible.

Psalm 115:2–7

Genesis 3:1

Revelation 22:17

In *Knowing the Father*, we see that the Bible never tries to prove that God exists; it simply asserts the fact of his existence as a self-evident reality. Even an Old Testament book like Esther, which does not actually mention God, clearly assumes that he exists.

Instead of defining God, the Bible introduces him. Its revelation is *personal*, rather than *propositional*, and reveals him in the context of relationships with ordinary people. The Bible uses new situations, fresh experiences and challenging events to pose questions about God's character – and to reveal the many ways that he communicates.

Exodus 15:1–18

Revelation 15:3

For example, the Song of Moses was composed immediately after Israel's miraculous escape from Egypt. The rhetorical question asked in Exodus 15:11 suggests that God's people had just been convinced that God was all-powerful and deserved their total allegiance. They did not stop to ask themselves whether other 'gods' really existed; it was enough for them to recognise that *Yahweh* had revealed his reality and power through their deliverance.

From the mighty crossing of the Red Sea, the Old Testament goes on to record a broad sweep of about 800 years of God's dealings with his people. Israel's defeats and decline did not lead its people to conclude that *Yahweh* was weak or uncaring, or even to think that he was only one among many different national gods. Instead, God's dealings with his people climax in the majestic revelation of Isaiah 44:6.

Isaiah 44:6

In particular, the Old Testament contains three ideas which distinguish Israel's understanding of God from that of other nations in those days. These ideas are fundamental to biblical revelation, and are still important today.

1.   God is not visible

All the nations around Israel depicted their gods in the shape of idols – usually as animals: the Canaanite god, *Baal*, for example, was generally portrayed as a young bull. Throughout the Old Testament, Israel was always under considerable pressure to turn *Yahweh* into a visible idol.

Exodus 32:1–35

Deuteronomy 9:7–21

Exodus 32:1–35 and Deuteronomy 9:7–21 report that, while Moses was on Mount Sinai listening to God and receiving the Law, the people were busy melting their jewellery and reshaping it into a calf which they intended to worship. They thought that it would be easier to talk to a god that they could see.

The issue of visible gods became a greater problem after the one nation divided into Israel and Judah. 1 Kings 12:28–33 describes how King Jeroboam of Israel erected golden bulls at Bethel and Dan to enlist the support of his Canaanite subjects. Jeroboam justified this by suggesting that the idols were similar to the ark of the covenant in Jerusalem – which gave a visible form to the invisible God. 1 Kings 14:7–16 is God's grim last word about King Jeroboam.

1 Kings 12:28–33

1 Kings 14:7–16

The truth that God is invisible permeates the Old Testament. Exodus 20:4–5; Deuteronomy 5:8–9 & Isaiah 44:9–20 demonstrate just how wrong it was to create any statue or idol for worship.

Exodus 20:4–5

Deuteronomy 5:8–9

Isaiah 44:9–20

This has clear implications for our 'listening' today. *Yahweh* simply does not communicate with us through any inanimate, human-made objects, and we must not think that religious trinkets or statues can ever be used to help us to hear him more clearly, or to bring us any closer to him. God is still firmly opposed to *any* form of idols.

2.   God is not a natural force

Many nations around Israel used gods to explain the seasons and the weather. They thought, for example, that thunder and lightning could be identified as one god, and that the annual flooding of the Nile was another. Many nations linked their gods to the cycle of rains which watered their crops.

But *Yahweh*, the living God of Israel, is beyond nature, and not part of nature. He is the Creator and Sustainer of all things, and not to be personally identified with any aspect of his creation.

Although the Old Testament sometimes uses poetic imagery to describe God in terms of different natural forces – such as light and fire – God himself cannot be identified with any feature of the natural world. We see this, for example, in Exodus 19:18; Deuteronomy 4:32–36; 1 Kings 19:11–13; Psalm 104:1–7 & Ezekiel 1:24–28.

Exodus 19:18

Deuteronomy 4:32–36

1 Kings 19:11–13

Psalm 104:1–7

Ezekiel 1:24–28

Again, this has obvious relevance for receiving revelation from God. Some people suppose that they are closer to God in a church, in a human-made building; while others think that they draw close to him in a wood or field. Neither idea is true. They both originate in pagan ideas about gods which Israel had to resist, and which the church still has to challenge today.

Of course, we do often hear God speak when we are in human-made buildings and when we are out in the open air. But we do not hear him *because* we are in such a place.

3.   God is not abstract

As *Yahweh* is far beyond human description, and is much greater than the sum of all human intelligence, the Bible never tries to define him in human words. No physical or philosophical formula can ever be the key to understanding God, to gaining access to the depths of his being, or to listening to his mind and counsel.

The Old Testament does not attempt to analyse God, or even to wonder what he can be made of. This sort of abstract approach was alien to Israel's concept of God. Unlike other nations around them, the people of Israel did not think about *Yahweh* metaphysically; rather, they explored his relevance to their human life and experience.

We can define someone by describing their appearance – their age, colour, height, weight and so on. This may provide an accurate mental picture, but it reveals little of any note. It is far more useful to describe someone by relating how they respond in particular circumstances, by outlining their abilities and personality, by reporting an incident which illustrates their character, by describing the sorts of things they say. This is how the people of Israel describe God in the Old Testament.

What is God like?

The *whole* Bible is *God's* attempt to introduce *himself* to us. All 39 books of the Old Testament, and all 27 of the New, describe the different ways that he has revealed himself to his people.

The early chapters of Genesis describe God's revelation through creation. From then until the book of Nehemiah, the Bible contains a series of long and complicated historical accounts which cover almost two thousand years of God's dealings with the nation of Israel – from the time of Abraham in the Middle Bronze Age, through to the Persian Empire, and on to a couple of centuries before Christ.

As well as these revelations through *creation* and *history*, the Old Testament also contains many books which show how God relates to the more ordinary circumstances of everyday life – both to *society-in-general*, and to the *personal life* of individual people. We see these elements in books like Ruth, Esther, Job, Jonah, Proverbs and Psalms, and in all the prophetic books from Isaiah to Malachi.

By using a great variety of styles of literature, the Old Testament offers many different perspectives on the way that God communicates with his people. There are, however, three main divine themes which dominate the Old Testament; and these are basic to Israel's relationship with *Yahweh*.

If we want to listen to God, we must appreciate these themes; for we need to know what *Yahweh* is like to understand how he speaks to us.

GOD IS ACTIVE

The Old Testament declares that God is encountered throughout Israel's national life. In fact, it is only because God is active that history has any meaning. Life is not a meaningless cycle of haphazard events. It has a purpose and design which is based in God's character, and God communicates through historical events.

From Noah's day to Nehemiah's, the Old Testament reveals that *Yahweh* controls history and that he communicates his will through it.

Everything that happens – bad and good – is part of God's purpose for his people. This is the basic conviction which shapes the way that the Old Testament understands and interprets events.

We can say that *God's activity* is expressed in four main Old Testament beliefs.

1.   God actively chooses his people

From one viewpoint, Abraham's migration from Mesopotamia was merely typical of many similar migrations at that time. From the biblical viewpoint, however, Abraham's journey was part of God's plan.

God's Genesis 12:3 promise was the driving force in Abraham's life. This shows that *Yahweh* wanted to use Abraham to share his divine

Genesis 12:3

love with the *whole* world. This belief dominates the story of Israel's development, and is the heart of biblical faith.

Some people try to explain Israel's exodus from Egypt by referring to the geography and demography of the region. From the biblical angle, however, the exodus is simply a revelation of God himself. Without his active intervention, it could not have taken place.

Throughout the Bible, we read that the people of Israel continually referred back to the story of the exodus to remind themselves of God's character. It underlined to them that *Yahweh* was active in history, and revealed invaluable insights into the nature of his activity.

2.   God actively loves his people

The stories in Exodus not only underline God's active choosing of his people, they also stress his active love for them. The slaves were weak, their leaders were inexperienced and the Egyptians were powerful: if Israel had relied on human resources, the exodus would have failed.

Deuteronomy
26:7–8 Passages like Deuteronomy 26:7–8 show that succeeding generations of Jews looked to a listening, loving God as the only possible explanation of the exodus. For them, the exodus was not just a clear demonstration of God's power, it was also a communicating experience – a revelation – of his love.

The exodus focused on people who were past helping themselves; and the Bible uses this fact to keep on reminding us that God has a special interest in caring for the victims of unjust oppression. God gives us his love so that we can share it with the needy and hurting: he does not provide it only for our personal blessing.

When we know what God is really like, we begin to appreciate the eternal divine principles which lie behind his words. We do not need, for example, to hear an audible voice directing us to care for the oppressed, because the Scriptures reveals that this is God's heart for all time. We can say that this principle is part of God's *general will*.

We do need, however, to listen for his instructions as to *how* we should express his care in each situation – for his *particular will*.

As we see in Parts Three and Four, God's divine principles are set firm in the Scriptures, but he applies them – by the Spirit – in particular loving ways which can vary in different situations.

3.   God's activity is infinitely powerful

Divine power dominates all God's actions and communications in the Scriptures. *Yahweh* does not act powerfully only to save his people from slavery, he also controls all the powers of nations and nature.

God spoke to Moses through the burning bush. He cursed Egypt with plagues. He parted rivers and seas. He provided food and water in the desert. And he used the surrounding pagan nations to accomplish his plans – sometimes of judgement, sometimes of blessing, but always to reveal his loving purpose to his chosen people.

When we listen to God, we must always remember that it is the all-loving, all-powerful God who is speaking. This awareness should transform our desire to listen to God, our persistence and patience in listening to him, and our confidence in the effectiveness of his words.

4.   God's activity is always perfectly just

The Law is another Old Testament sign of God's activity. This shows that God communications are always in accordance with his own standards of justice, and are never arbitrary or unpredictable. Morality and justice are always central to God's dealings with his people.

Exodus 3:2–22 & Isaiah 6:1–5 describe the divine visions that Moses and Isaiah received in the wilderness and the temple. These passages report that it was not the supernatural aspects of the experience which impressed them. Instead, they responded to God's revelation by confessing their personal inadequacy in the face of his moral perfection.

Exodus 3:2–22

Isaiah 6:1–5

This suggests that we must face up to the demands of God's justice when he speaks to us – whether in temple, history, nature, or everyday experience. When we listen to God, we must expect him to deal with our sin and short-comings whenever he gives us his instructions.

God's activity

God's active *choosing, loving, power* and *justice* dominate the entire Old Testament. As the generations passed, however, Israel and Judah seemed to become increasingly insignificant nations to be scrabbled over by the great empires around them. To most ordinary Jews, it must have seemed that these foreign powers were in control, not God.

Many modern believers struggle with God's promises because they are confronted by considerable social pressures and personal problems. But this is not a new problem, for the people of Israel struggled in exactly the same way.

How practical were God's words to Abraham for people who lived in the shadow of great empires? How relevant were God's deeds in the exodus to Jewish slaves in Babylon? If Israel had been chosen by God, why were they not triumphant in all their battles? If God was in control, how could other nations have the upper hand?

The Old Testament prophets gave a clear answer to these questions – an answer which is desperately relevant to our struggles with listening to God and understanding his will. The prophets taught that God's self-revelation and love imposed great responsibilities. The people of Israel would prosper while they were faithful. But they would need to return to God for forgiveness whenever they became unfaithful.

Genesis 12:3

The people of Israel imagined that God's revelations to *them* demonstrated that they were his favourites. But the prophets knew that *Yahweh*'s intention was the salvation and blessing of *all* people, as God had promised to Abraham in Genesis 12:3. Although Israel had been specially favoured, and had experienced great acts of power, God's love and power could operate only within the context of God's justice.

It is no different for us. Our privileges as sons and daughters of God *increase* our responsibility to demonstrate God's justice; and our experience of salvation *magnifies* our duty to witness to all the families of the earth about God's saving love and power.

Isaiah 31:4–5

Jeremiah 7:1–15

The prophets' knowledge of God's will – through their prophetic listening – often brought them into conflict with Israel's rulers. The advice they gave may appear, at times, to be contradictory. In Isaiah 31:4–5, for example, the prophet advised the king that God would protect the nation from an Assyrian invasion. While, a few generations later, Jeremiah proclaimed the opposite – in Jeremiah 7:1–15.

Jeremiah 24:1–10

But although these prophetic announcements were different, the underlying prophetic principle was the same. Those people who set themselves against God – whether Assyria or Judah – would be judged. This means that the Babylonian exile and the destruction of Jerusalem were as much a communication from God as the exodus from Egypt. We see this clearly in Jeremiah 24:1–10.

This was hard for Jewish people to understand. They thought that God was on their side. But the whole Bible explains why God – at times – appears to abandon his people. From Genesis to Malachi, from Matthew to Revelation, the eternal divine principle is plain: disobedience leads to judgement, but this is always wrapped in grace and forgiveness. It is still the same today.

Prophetic passages like Psalm 47 and Amos 1:3–2:5 reminded the Jews that – despite the appearance – God was in control of *all* nations, and not just of Israel. Isaiah 44:1–20; 45:1–4; 47:1–15 & 49:6 declare that *Yahweh* is the God of the *whole* world.

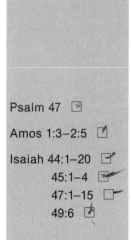

Psalm 47

Amos 1:3–2:5

Isaiah 44:1–20

45:1–4

47:1–15

49:6

The Jewish exile, therefore, did not communicate God's defeat, it revealed his justice. God's power was not diminished and his love was not exhausted, for he promised to raise a Persian deliverer for his people – and to fulfil his promise to Abraham through his Servant who would be a light to the nations.

This brief description of God's activity shows that 'listening to God' is not a spiritual exercise which is somehow removed from everyday life. Throughout history, God's people have encountered the active, speaking, self-revealing God in practical situations as glorious as the exodus and as ghastly as the exile.

No matter whether our personal circumstances are joyful, terrible, or just dull, God is always with us. He is speaking to us. He is revealing his love to us. He is communicating his purposes. He is breathing life-giving, hope-bringing words to us.

GOD IS PERSONAL

The Old Testament does not only stress that God is *active*, it also emphasises that he is fully *personal*. We consider God's personal nature more fully in *Knowing the Father*. Although *Yahweh* does communicate through the great sweep of history, he does not relate to people in an impersonal, mechanical way. He is deeply interested in the world and humanity, and is never distant from people and their needs.

All the great events of the Old Testament stress that God is not capricious or unpredictable. He always acts in accordance with his own nature. He does not manipulate events for his own advantage; rather, he acts in grace to demonstrate his great love. He does not impose his will to achieve his own ends; instead, he acts because he is concerned for people and for their good.

Although the Old Testament concentrates on the way that God communicates personally with his people Israel, and shows how he speaks to them as a nation – as a group of people – it is wrong to imagine that God deals with people only in large numbers.

The scriptural revelation of God is built upon God's personal concern for Abraham and Sarah when they are living in a hostile land. The Bible then shows that God also cares deeply for Hagar and Ishmael – for an Egyptian slave and her child – when they are expelled from Abraham's household. Next, God protects Joseph, saving him from his family and the Egyptians. Later on, we see God's great personal concern for individual pagans like Rahab, Ruth, Naomi and the people of Ninevah.

Many of the prayers and hymns in the Psalms reveal how worshippers in Israel knew that God was personally interested in the details of their ordinary lives. We see this, for example, in Psalms 13; 17; 23; 35; 51; 69; 86 & 139. And most of the prophets stress the importance of individual commitment to the personal God.

Personal images

The Old Testament emphasis on God's personal nature is seen particularly clearly in the names, titles and images used to describe and identify God. We consider these in detail in *Knowing the Father*.

The book of Hosea uses the imagery of broken personal relation-ships to show how God relates personally – and the pain that he endures by communicating in this way. Passages like Exodus 4:22; Isaiah 1:2; 49:15; 66:13; Jeremiah 31:32; Ezekiel 16:3–8; Hosea 2:14–23 & 11:4 illustrate the personal way that God relates to his people.

Although the Old Testament does describe God in terms of family relationships, it more commonly portrays him as the ruler of his people: he is the king, the lord, the shepherd, the master, the leader in battle. Of course, every picture of God is an attempt to describe a divine person who is beyond human description. Every single name or image of God suggests a particular aspect of his character; but each name must be understood in the context of the totality of all his names.

Genesis
12:10–20
21:9–21
39:2–23
Joshua 2:12–24
6:22–25
Jonah 4:11

Psalms 13
17
23
35
51
69
86
139

Exodus 4:22
Isaiah 1:2
49:15
66:13
Jeremiah 31:32
Ezekiel 16:3–8
Hosea 2:14–23
11:4

If we concentrate on those Old Testament passages which refer to God as a husband or father, we miss the sense of awe and wonder which fills the Old Testament. But if we focus only on God as a master or monarch we may suggest that he is a harsh dictator.

God is very different from men and women, but the Old Testament declares that God's perfection and humanity's imperfection are bridged by his loving actions of salvation and blessing. And these actions are meaningful precisely because God is not a force or an abstract will – he is a person, with all this implies about his speaking and our listening.

GOD IS HIDDEN

The Old Testament is dominated by the conviction that God's nature is communicated by his dealings with his people. Throughout the Scriptures, men and women meet God in the ordinary events of everyday life. It is clear that God is personally related to the people of earth, rather than merely being a remote deity of the heavens.

Many people struggle with this today. They do not see events like the exodus. They do not have experiences like Moses in the wilderness and Isaiah in the temple. And so they wonder whether the Old Testament teaching about God has any relevance to their modern lives.

The Old Testament deals with these doubts by adding a third element to its portrayal of God. It presents him not only as active in *history* and *personal experience*, but also as *hidden* from people in the Old Testament as he seems to be to so many today.

People in Israel often found it difficult to find any trace of God when they needed his help to make sense of their lives. The visible facts of history did not always suggest to them that God was all-powerful and all-loving. The details of their personal lives did not always indicate that a living, personal God was communicating lovingly with them.

In fact, the opposite often seemed to be the case; as evil and suffering seemed to dominate their lives as much as they seem to influence ours.

Few believers find it difficult to hear God and to understand his will when they are experiencing miraculous events and obvious blessing – when it is patently clear that God is closer than any human friend.

But our spiritual lives are not always filled with dramatic miracles and supernatural experiences. There are times when God does appear to be hidden and it is hard to hear his voice. As we see in *Living Faith*, this is an essential part of the development of mature faith.

The Old Testament makes it clear that there are times when God seems far from powerful and active, when he is lost in the depths of human despair. This is particularly plain in the book of Psalms.

Some Psalms celebrate God's mighty works; but many express sorrow, bewilderment and dismay; while others complain that the realities of life seem inconsistent with the reports of God's past deeds. Even those Psalms which exude confidence in God also recognise that he has to be sought in times of the deepest darkness.

Personal alienation

When we read the Bible, it is tempting to concentrate on stories which communicate God's love and power. The Bible, however, also records the struggles that people had with God's hiddenness. For example:

Genesis 15:6 ☐
18:16–33 ☐

Exodus 5:22–23 ☐
33:11 ☐

1 Kings 18:1–40 ☐
19:1–18 ☐

Jeremiah 1:4 ☐
11:18–23 ☐
12:1–6 ☐
15:10–21 ☐
17:14–18 ☐
18:18–23 ☐
20:7–18 ☐

- *Abraham* was a man of tremendous faith, but he often found God's intentions puzzling. At times, Abraham thought they were so hard to reconcile with God's nature that he argued with God.

- *Moses* experienced God in an exceptionally intimate way, but his life was full of questions and complaints as he struggled to reconcile God's promises with what he observed around him.

- *Elijah* won a famous victory in the name of God at Carmel, and experienced God's power in quite extraordinary ways. Yet it seemed to him that God immediately deserted him; he doubted God's love and power, and wanted to die.

- *Jeremiah* knew that he had been chosen as a prophet, and that he was loved and protected, yet God seemed reluctant to support his prophetic announcements. Nothing happened for twenty-five years after he had obediently announced the destruction of Jerusalem, and Jeremiah wondered why he had been born.

The hiddenness of God is a major theme in the books of Job and Ecclesiastes. They show that God is known not in the imagination but in the reality of personal encounter. Job appealed to God to speak to him – and he eventually did, but not in the way that Job had expected.

Job's listening reminded him that – no matter how difficult it is to understand life's bitterest experiences, or how hard it is to perceive God at work – God really is there.

Believers who resist easy answers, who persist in seeking God, and in listening to him, *will* meet him and *will* hear his words.

National disaster

The fall of Jerusalem to Nebuchadnezzar shattered Israel's expectations of God. It seemed that God's promises had failed, that he was silent, that *Yahweh* was no longer with them.

Much of the Old Testament reflects the puzzlement of people who wonder how this disaster could happen to God's people in a world which is controlled by God. Through the prophets, we see that the people were called to understand the Jewish exile in Babylon by holding two different ideas together in tension.

1. There had been great crises in the past, and God's mighty power had often burst in to change the lives of those who were least expecting it. The exodus had not been an unnecessary blessing, it had been God's answer to slavery and the threat of extinction.

2. The Jews were suffering as a result of their nation's disobedience. A just God could not ignore the moral shortcomings and social injustice of his people. But even though God's justice seemed to outweigh his love, the prophets announced that God would be faithful to his promises and that he would eventually bless Israel.

Quite often, however, the Old Testament does not try to explain why God appears to be silent and hidden from his people. Instead, it gives a clear and practical message to those individuals who are finding it hard to hear God in their own lives.

As men and women in the Bible contemplated their suffering, they were forced to confess that God's ways were puzzling and perplexing. Like us, they had to learn that *Yahweh's* perfect pattern rarely conforms to our imperfect expectations.

Alongside this, however, Old Testament people also affirmed that God had communicated powerfully in their history and personal experience. This assured them that God was active – even though he was presently hidden by the gloom of their human situation.

REVELATION PRINCIPLES

We have seen that the biblical revelation of God is set in the context of his personal relationships with his people. This means that we learn about receiving revelation, about listening to God, by studying his relationships.

We discover the depths of his character by seeing how he communicates with people in a variety of challenging situations. By faith, we then apply these truths to our lives.

The Old Testament makes two major assumptions about God which determine the way that he communicates with people. These two assumptions are fundamental to our understanding of revelation *and* to the practical way that we listen to him.

1.   God acts in grace

The Old Testament often uses human images to describe God – it suggests that he has hands and eyes, that he cries and laughs, and so on. Despite this, it is clear that God is very different from people.

His actions are not rationalisations of human behaviour, and he cannot be bullied or cajoled or manipulated. Whenever God communicates with people, it is because *he* has taken the initiative.

The divine initiative of grace is central to the biblical understanding of revelation. Every relationship with God, every communication from God, is based entirely on his personal action in grace.

God has chosen to commit himself to *all* humanity, and we have seen that he called Abraham to enable him to achieve this end. God acted entirely freely in this, with the sole motive of sharing his gracious love with all the people who live in his world.

At every significant point in the salvation story, the Old Testament stresses that God's grace is the starting point for any contact with God or any revelation from God.

For example, the exodus occurs because God sees the plight of his people and takes pity on them – not because the slaves ask for it. Individual men and women enjoy fellowship with God because of the gracious initiative of his love – not because they have a right to fellowship or some sort claim on God. Nobody can create a sense of God's presence or voice, he must always break in from outside.

We consider the important relationship between God's gracious initiative and our listening response in Part Four.

2.   God speaks

It is impossible to read the Old Testament without recognising its constant insistence that God speaks. The first two facts we learn about God in Genesis 1 are that he is a *creator* and a *speaker* – and that his speaking and his creating are intertwined with each other.

This might suggest to some people that God speaks or communicates essentially *through* his mighty acts. And, indeed, the Old Testament does often claim that God has communicated through his actions in history and personal experience. We must recognise, however, that God's speaking is not the same as his acting.

For Israel, the events of the exodus were a wonderful revelation of God's nature and will – yet they communicated little about *Yahweh* to the Egyptians. Something 'extra' is needed to change a general divine action into a personal divine revelation.

One of the most remarkable facts about the Old Testament is that the prophets of Israel did not only interpret God's actions for the people in retrospect, they also announced them in advance. For example:

- *Amos* denounced Samarian society, and declared that it would soon end, when there was no sign of any such event. In fact, at that time, the nation had never been so prosperous.

- *Jeremiah* announced the destruction of Jerusalem, and the people thought that he was mad to suggest such an implausible thing. Nothing seemed less likely to contemporary observers.

- *Moses* announced the exodus while the Hebrew people were still in slavery to the most powerful nation on earth.

The prophets persisted with their messages, often in the face of ridicule and persecution, because they were convinced that what they were saying was God's message to the people – and because they believed that God acted essentially *through* his speaking.

They knew that their obedient, active speaking of the words that they had heard was a vital part of his creative process.

Listening to 'the God-who-speaks-to-create' was the heart of the Old Testament prophetic ministry. And the faithful proclamation of God's Word – usually through his servants, the Spirit-anointed prophets – was the normal precursor to God's creative activity.

As we see in *Living Faith* and *Ministry in the Spirit*, this pattern has not changed. The only difference is that, since Pentecost, the prophetic ministry has been open to *all* God's people – which is why listening to the communicating God should be a fundamental part of the lives of all prophetic, Spirit-anointed believers today.

This partnership between 'believers speaking God's words' and 'God's creative actions' is the reason why we are focusing on 'prophetic' listening, and are examining 'listening to God' in the context of the broad prophetic ministry. This underlines that our listening is not a passive activity; instead, it is a vital part of God's 'speaking-to-act' ministry.

Yahweh, the living God of Israel, is not a static remote being who is irrelevant to the lives of ordinary people. He is the all-loving, all-powerful, all-grace God who speaks-and-acts *so that* all the families of earth might have an abundant and meaningful relationship with him and with each other. And, when we listen to him, we become part of his dynamic revelatory activity.

Our calling to listen to God is both an extraordinary privilege and an awesome responsibility. Like the prophets of old, we are called into *Yahweh's* holy presence to hear his thoughts, and are then sent into the world to speak his words – so that his creative power can transform the broken and hurting lives around us.

PART THREE

the word of god

The God of the Bible is the God who speaks. He is not a dumb idol who is unable to communicate with his people, nor an automaton who merely responds to requests. Rather, *Yahweh* is the all-gracious God who always takes the *initiative*: he speaks, we listen; and he reveals himself to all those who will learn to listen attentively to him. We see this, for example, in Psalm 115:2–7; Isaiah 46:5–10; Habakkuk 2:18–20 & 1 Corinthians 12:2.

The Bible teaches that God communicates with us through:

- *creation* – Psalm 19:1–6; Romans 1:18–21

- *historical events* – Psalm 103:7; Jeremiah 9:12–16

- *human conscience* – Romans 2:14–15

- *holy scripture* – Psalm 19:7–11; 2 Timothy 3:16–17; 2 Peter 1:19–21

- *prophetic servants* – 1 Corinthians 12:3, 10; 1 Thessalonians 5:20

- *Jesus Christ* – John 1:18; Hebrews 1:1–3

God takes the initiative and speaks through these different means essentially to reveal *himself* to us. He does this so that we can know him, and can fulfil our purposes as men and women in his world.

The general scriptural name for God's means of communication is his 'Word', and we consider this in some detail in *Living Faith*. If we want to listen to God – if we want to hear his 'voice' and know what he is 'saying' – we need to listen for his 'Word'.

The Old and the New Testaments often refer to 'God's Word', 'the Word of the Lord', 'your Word', and so on: it is important, therefore, that we understand exactly what the Bible means by 'the Word'.

DABAR

Psalm 119 ☐

In the Old Testament, the Hebrew word *dabar* is used to refer to 'the Word' of God. *Dabar* usually means a *spoken* communication from God; it refers to a *written* communication from him only in Psalm 119 – where it is used as a synonym for the first five books of the Old Testament.

Matthew 3:17 ☐

When we say that God 'speaks' we are using a metaphor. God is a spiritual being who does not literally possess a throat, tongue, mouth and vocal chords. He does not normally communicate with an audible voice which we hear with our physical ears: events like those in Matthew 3:17 are rare. Instead, God usually 'speaks' his Word into our spirits so that we hear him spiritually.

Dabar is often part of the Old Testament expression, 'the Word of the Lord came to'. This underlines God's gracious initiative. His Word first comes to us; we then, in gratitude, respond by turning to his Word with loving openness and gospel obedience.

Dabar literally means 'that which lies behind', and points to the divine reality which is behind the words that we 'hear' in our spirits. This 'self-revelation' is the essence of biblical teaching about God's 'Word' – it is vital that we appreciate this. The use of *dabar* proves that God 'speaks' to us essentially to reveal *himself* to us. This means that we should listen to God primarily to know *him* better – and only secondarily to receive direction for ourselves.

In Old Testament times, a person's *dabar* – their word – was regarded both as being an extension of that person's personality, and also as having a substantive existence of its own. This means that God's Word is a divine self-revelation of his holy personality, which – when 'spoken' – then continues to exist in its own right for eternity.

Self-revelation

Many modern believers say that 'the Word is the Bible'. Unfortunately, this can suggest that the Word is restricted to the Bible: it is more accurate to say that 'the written Word is the Bible'.

As the Word's chief function is the revelation of God's eternal nature, it must be expressed in several complementary forms to communicate his nature at all accurately. The eternal fullness of the Word is far greater than can ever be expressed in a finite form, so the Scriptures are the essential written form of God's Word, and not the totality of the Word.

Some leaders stress that the Bible is a 'guide book for living' and a 'rule book for humanity'; they promise success when we live by biblical requirements. But too great an emphasis on this truth can mean that we miss the central purpose of the Bible – which is to reveal God to us.

We misunderstand God's purposes when we read the Bible simply to receive instructions. God has given us his written Word so that we may know him better, and may be drawn deeper into his life.

Sadly, a right emphasis on the importance and centrality of the Scriptures has led some believers into a legalistic relationship with the Bible rather than a living relationship with God.

Right thinking about the full Word – which is founded on God's essential self-revelation – leads to many helpful attitudes. For example:

- *we begin to appreciate why Jesus and the Scriptures are both called 'the Word'*

- *we realise why the Bible invests the Word with God's divine authority and characteristics – as in Deuteronomy 12:32; Psalm 103:20; Isaiah 40:8; 55:11 & 1 Peter 1:23–25*

- *we approach our listening to God – and our proclamation of his Word – in a much more biblical 'God-centred' way*

Deuteronomy
    12:32 ☐

Psalm 103:20 ☐

Isaiah 40:8 ☐
        55:11 ☐

1 Peter 1:23–25 ☐

LOGOS & RHEMA

Dabar is used to describe both specific communications from God and his total self-revelation. In the New Testament, however, two different Greek words are used. *Rhema* refers to particular communications from God, and *logos* points to his total self-revelation. We consider this more fully in *Living Faith*.

We know that God has supremely revealed himself to humanity through *Jesus* and through *the Bible*; and we can therefore think of Jesus as God's 'Personal Word' and the Bible as God's 'Written Word'. This is why they are both identified as God's *logos*.

Jesus

Once we realise that Jesus is 'the Word of God' – the distinct, total self-revelation of God – we can start to think about the relationship between 'listening to God' and 'the Word of God' more biblically.

Listening to God is not only for educated people who have an intellectual grasp of the Bible. It is part of a living relationship with Jesus which is open to all people, regardless of their intellectual ability.

This does not mean that the Scriptures are unimportant – far from it. But it is possible to read the Bible with only our human minds and to study it with only our personal intellects. Many people do this and profess that, through this, they know God's Word. But we can only truly listen to God in our spirits, with the help of the Holy Spirit.

Of course, *logos* does not point only to Jesus; it is also used in the New Testament to describe the revealed will of God in much the same way as the phrase 'the Word of God' is used in the Old Testament. It is used, for example, to describe:

- *a direct revelation from Jesus* – 1 Thessalonians 4:15

- *the sum of all God's utterances* – Mark 7:13; John 10:35

- *the good news or 'gospel' about Jesus – delivered with his authority and made effective by his power* – Acts 8:25; 13:26, 49; 14:3; 15:7, 35, 36; 16:32; 19:10; 1 Corinthians 1:18; 2 Corinthians 2:17; 4:2; 5:19; 6:7; Galatians 6:6; Ephesians 1:13; Philippians 2:16; Colossians 1:5; Hebrews 5:13

Logos is often used to describe the 'good news', the 'gospel'. In the New Testament, the gospel is essentially a presentation of Jesus himself. He is the Word which is preached in total dependence on the power of the Holy Spirit.

We can say that, in the early church, 'the Word' always meant a self-revelatory message from God, in Christ, through the Spirit. This had to be preached and ministered with the help of the Spirit – and obeyed by those who heard it – as if it were an audible word from-and-about Christ himself.

Rhema

In *Living Faith*, we establish that *rhema* points to specific words from God, as opposed to the totality of God's Word represented by *logos*. The *rhema* of God, however, is not something different from the *logos* of God, it is an aspect of the *logos*. By a *rhema* word, God highlights one element within his *logos*; it is the 'word within the Word' which is his direct word for a particular situation at one special moment.

Every word from God agrees with both the full self-revelatory *logos* of God *and* also with every individual *rhema* of God. This means that every divine communication – every prophecy, promise, prompting and so on – is always fully consistent with the whole *logos* of God. It conforms with everything that we know about God through Christ and through the Scriptures, and also with all the *rhema* words of God which have ever been uttered.

This shows the importance of testing everything which people claim to be a word or message from God. If every *rhema* word is a self-revelation of God, it means that every word must be fully consistent with all we know about God, all we know about Jesus, and with the full revelation of the Holy Scriptures.

When God, by the Spirit, 'speaks' his *rhema* word into our spirits, it is as if he uses a divine searchlight. By a *rhema* word, God pinpoints one aspect of his *logos* word and reveals his 'now' word – that aspect of his own character which is supremely relevant to our situation.

We see examples of a *rhema* word in: Matthew 4:4; 26:75; Mark 14:72; Luke 1:38; 2:29; 3:2; 5:5; 24:8; John 5:47; 6:63; 8:20; 8:47; 12:47–48; 14:10; 15:7; 17:8; Acts 2:14; 10:37; 11:16; Romans 10:8, 17–18; Ephesians 6:17; 1 Peter 1:25; Jude 1:17 and Revelation 17:17.

Matthew 4:4 ☐
26:75 ☐
Mark 14:72 ☐
Luke 1:38 ☐
2:29 ☐
3:2 ☐
5:5 ☐
24:8 ☐
John 5:47 ☐
6:63 ☐
8:20 ☐
8:47 ☐
12:47–48 ☐
14:10 ☐
15:7 ☐
17:8 ☐
Acts 2:14 ☐
10:37 ☐
11:16 ☐
Romans 10:8 ☐
10:17–18 ☐
Ephesians 6:17 ☐
1 Peter 1:25 ☐
Jude 1:17 ☐
Revelation 17:17 ☐

THE WORD OF GOD

Because God communicates with us by his Word, it is important for us to try to understand how the Word works.

2 Timothy 3:16–17 reveals that all Scripture comes to us on God's breath. Most English translations of the Bible suggest that Scripture is 'inspired', but the Greek word *theopneustos* means 'God breathed'. This shows that the Scriptures are, in some special way, uniquely 'expired' by God's breath, by the Holy Spirit himself.

Passages like Psalm 33:6 and 2 Peter 1:19–21 also stress that God's Word comes by the Spirit, by God's breath. They show that, because the Word is God-breathed, it is the very word of God – it is 'the breath of his lips'.

More importantly, by using the present tense – 'is God-breathed' rather than 'was God-breathed' – 2 Timothy 3:16 also shows that the Scriptures were not merely breathed once-and-for-all when they were first written down, or when they were collected together. Instead, they are still being breathed by God to us by the Spirit.

The power of the Word

Whenever God 'breathes' his Word by the Spirit, it always expresses his holy nature and is always vested with his divine power and authority. The Word, therefore, simply must always achieve its purpose: what God 'speaks' will come to pass; we see this in, for example, Genesis 1:3, 6–7, 9, 11, 14–15, 20–22, 24, 26–27; 2 Chronicles 6:14–15; Isaiah 55:10–11 and Romans 4:18–21.

Hebrews 4:12 describes the Word as living, active, sharp. This verse teaches that God's *logos* accomplishes an inward, spiritual work in our lives. It exposes our thoughts and attitudes, cuts through the appearance of our outward behaviour to the reality of our 'heart', and penetrates deep into our spirits.

The inherent divine power of the Word is emphasised throughout the whole Bible. Both testaments reveal a great variety of ways that the whole Word of God ministers to men and women. We see, for example, that the God 'who speaks-to-act' brings through the Word:

- *faith* – Romans 10:17

- *new birth and new life* – James 1:18; 1 Peter 1:23

- *spiritual food* – 1 Peter 2:1–2; Matthew 4:4

- *revelation and direction* – Psalm 119:105, 130

- *cleansing and holiness* – Psalm 119:9; Ephesians 5:25–27; 2 Peter 1:1–4; John 15:3

- *reward and blessing* – Psalm 1:1–3; 19:11

- *healing* – Psalm 107:20

- *victory over sin* – Psalm 17:4; 119:11

- *victory over Satan* – Luke 4:4, 8, 12; Ephesians 6:17; 1 John 2:14; Revelation 12:11

- *freedom from judgement* – John 5:24; 12:47

God can use any element of his Word – Jesus, personally in the Spirit, the Scriptures, prophecy – to minister any of these gifts to us. It should be clear, however, that the Word operates with this extraordinary effectiveness only because it is an expression of God's personal nature and is filled with his personal divine power.

THE WRITTEN WORD

When we approach 'the Written Word' to listen to God, we must remember that its purpose is personal and relational: God breathes his Word so that *we* may *know* him.

Although the scriptural revelation of God is limited by its finite nature, the Bible is an infallible and as-full-as-possible record of God's Word to humanity. It has two important characteristics: just as 'the Personal Word' is both fully God and fully human, so 'the Written Word' is also the Word of God *and* the Word through humans.

We need to remember this when we read the Bible. 2 Peter 1:20–21 shows that the human writers of the Scriptures did not imagine their words; instead, they were inspired by the Spirit – they wrote what God

Romans 10:17 ☐

James 1:18 ☐

1 Peter 1:23 ☐
2:1–2 ☐

Matthew 4:4 ☐

Psalm 119:105 ☐
119:130 ☐
119:9 ☐

Ephesians
5:25–27 ☐

2 Peter 1:1–4 ☐

John 15:3 ☐

Psalm 1:1–3 ☐
19:11 ☐
107:20 ☐
17:4 ☐
119:11 ☐

Luke 4:4, 8, 12 ☐

Ephesians 6:17 ☐

1 John 2:14 ☐

Revelation 12:11 ☐

John 5:24 ☐
12:47 ☐

2 Peter 1:20–21 ☐

intended to be written. This is why the Bible really is God's Word about himself, and not human words about God. It contains 66 books which were written by at least 40 different authors over about 1,600 years; yet it all rings with one clear sound – the 'voice' of the Spirit.

2 Timothy 3:15–17 ☐

2 Timothy 3:15–17 reveals that the Written Word is 'useful'. It is, however, more accurate to translate the Greek word *ophelimos* as 'profitable', or 'advantageous', or – best of all – 'beneficial'. The use of *ophelimos* in 1 Timothy 4:8 shows that it refers to something which is practically 'beneficial' rather than something which is casually 'useful'.

2 Timothy 3:17 establishes that every part of the whole of the Bible is deeply beneficial. This means that we should not accept some sections and reject others. We should not dismiss one passage as irrelevant, or overlook another because we consider it boring. We dare not judge any part of God's Word; in fact, the Word judges us.

2 Timothy 3:15–17 shows that all Scripture – the whole Bible – is deeply beneficial for:

- *teaching - God provides the standard by which everything is measured*

- *rebuking – God shows us where we have gone wrong*

- *correcting – God sets us back on the right path*

- *training in righteousness – God teaches us how to stay on his right path*

This shows that the Written Word completely equips believers for every aspect of ministry and life. It guides us accurately, and we can trust it as the final and supreme authority for living.

If we are serious about listening to God, we will never depart from *all* Scripture – we will read, study, meditate, believe and act on *every* part of the Bible.

The Living Word

Hebrews 4:12 ☐

We have noted, however, that the Bible is not an external rule book. Hebrews 4:12 makes it clear that the Word is alive and active. More importantly, it shows that God's Word operates deep inside us – in our 'hearts', in our spirits.

We have also noted that the Word comes to us on God's breath, on the Spirit: this means that God speaks to us in our spirits through the Scriptures – he reveals himself and guides us by the Written Word.

This does not mean, however, that God will never communicate anything more than he has already said in the Scriptures. We all face many situations when the Bible does not distinguish between our different options, and we need the Spirit to speak to us specifically – in more detail than is possible in the Bible.

For example, God may call us through the Scriptures – perhaps through a passage like Genesis 12:1; Jonah 1:2 or Acts 16:9 – to go to a far nation with the gospel; but he clearly cannot direct us through the Scriptures to a particular African, South American or Asian nation.

Genesis 12:1 ☐

Jonah 1:2 ☐

Acts 16:9 ☐

His Word must come to us by the Spirit in another way than the Scriptures to guide us particularly and personally – but it will always confirm and amplify what God has already communicated to us through the Written Word.

Isaiah 58:11 is an important promise which was given to God's people many centuries before Jesus came in the flesh and the New Testament was written. It demonstrates that God's guidance is not limited to the Bible.

Isaiah 58:11 ☐

Of course, God does guide us generally and doctrinally by his Written Word, but he also guides us personally and particularly by his Personal Word: and this also comes to us by his breath, by his Spirit.

As we see in *Knowing the Spirit*, just before Jesus left the earth, he promised to send *allos parakletos* – another Counsellor who would be exactly the same as him. And Jesus guaranteed that this Counsellor would be with us *forever*.

The Spirit is just like Jesus, and comes alongside us to call to us. He comes to guide us personally and specifically – as well as generally and doctrinally. We see this in the reference in John 16:13 to 'all' truth.

John 16:13 ☐

This shows that to listen to the Spirit is to listen to Jesus, to learn from the Spirit is to learn from Jesus, to be led by the Spirit is to be led by Jesus – and so on.

Many Christians have sound doctrine, yet are powerless to live for God because they have not understood that doctrine is not a matter of the mind and the intellect alone. We do need to listen to the Written

Word, and the Holy Spirit will never contradict it; but we also need to listen to the Holy Spirit – directly and personally. We consider these aspects of listening in Part Seven to Nine.

Superstitions

Listening to God through the Word and the Spirit is as far removed as possible from being guided by superstitions. An increasing number of people look to various forms of astrology for guidance, but these are superstitious and evil – and can, at times, even be manifestations of the evil one.

This does not mean that every person who has ever glanced at a newspaper horoscope needs to have a demon cast out! These things are superstitious, they are opposed to God's way of revelation, and – as such – they are used by the enemy to distract us from the discipline of listening to God and to attract us to his evil schemes.

However, when people persist in using some form of astrology, and *start to depend on it*, they leave themselves wide open to demonic influence. Even then, as we see in *Ministry in the Spirit*, we need the spiritual gift of the discerning of spirits to know what to do in any ministry situation.

Isaiah 47:13–14 ☐

1 Corinthians
        12:3 ☐

1 John 4:1–6 ☐

We must always take care to distinguish between listening to God and being misled by listening to the evil one. The enemy is a deceiver and a liar: he is opposed to God and God's people, and God is opposed to him and his methods of communication. We see this in Isaiah 47:13–14; 1 Corinthians 12:3 and 1 John 4:1–6.

All forms of divination, and all occultic or spiritistic guidance, are an abomination to God. In themselves, they are useless – they are mere 'props' of the hidden powers which are behind them.

As Christian believers, we are not to seek guidance by these means; instead, we are to approach God to listen to him – through his Personal Word and his Written Word – so that we know him much better and can share in his holy activities.

PART FOUR

the will of god

In *Knowing the Father*, we consider the will of the Father in some detail. We note that:

- *Jesus' relationship with his Father is characterised by complete trust and radical obedience*

- *'faith' is an almost identical scriptural concept to 'obedience' – to believe in God is to obey him; to obey God is to believe him*

- *biblical obedience, or 'gospel obedience', is always a response to God's grace and never a condition for grace*

The gospel proclaims that the Father welcomes us exactly as we are – as returning children, in all our unworthiness – and that our response to the Father's grace should be grateful obedience. We do not obey him to earn his gracious forgiveness.

The good news is that we are received by God without any pre-conditions; but we should never forget that we are returning to the Father's home and family where the Father is lord and should be obeyed.

Gospel obedience

In *Knowing the Father*, we establish that gospel obedience is more an *enabled obedience* than a required obedience. The Father does not make impossible demands and then stand back to watch us fail; instead, he gives us the Son and the Spirit by whom he enables us to obey him.

Furthermore, we see that gospel obedience is *personal obedience* to 'Abba', and not obedience to a code of general principles and detailed regulations. Romans 12:1–2 shows that gospel obedience is quite different from an attempt to live by Christian principles, or to abide by the Ten Commandments, or to implement the Sermon on the Mount.

Romans 12:1–2 ☐

It is plain that Jesus did not live by a programme or principles; he lived from minute-to-minute by discerning what particular form the consistent will of God was taking in each and every situation he faced.

He knew, for example, that healing was God's *general-and-ultimate will* for everyone; but he needed to understand God's *particular will* to know what to say to each sick person he met. John 5:1–15 shows that he discerned it was God's particular will to heal, through him, just one of a multitude of sick people on that day at that place.

John 5:1–15 ☐

And Acts 16:6–10 records how Paul was restrained by the Spirit from going one way to preach, and then from going another way, and then was directed God's particular way. Paul knew that it was God's *general will* for him to preach the gospel to the Gentiles, but he needed to understand God's *particular will* for his ministry at that time.

Acts 16:6–10 ☐

It is exactly this 'personally guided, particular obedience' to God's will which we need to follow in our lives – hence the great importance of listening to God to hear and understand his particular, moment-by-moment will for our lives. Just as it is the work of the Holy Spirit to reveal God's Personal and Written Word to us, so too it is his work to reveal God's particular will to us.

The priority of God's will

In *Knowing the Father*, we establish that the Father's will always has priority over our human will in his call to obedience: infinite grace is God's initiative, and gospel obedience is our response.

The divine order is clear: the Father initiates, we respond. Before we move one pace towards God, even while we are still saying 'No' to him, the Father comes to us in his Son in free-and-lavish grace. This is true in every area of the spiritual life.

Throughout this *Sword of the Spirit* series, we continually seek to stress this important principle. For example, we show repeatedly that:

- *God's will always has priority*

- *grace must be either first-and-foremost or it ceases to be grace*

- *God's faith, the Spirit's anointing, the gifts and ministries of the Spirit, are all given in the context of God's lavish grace*

- *any divine conditions – like gospel obedience – are a grateful human response to grace, not requirements for grace*

It should be obvious that this has considerable implications for the way that we listen to God. If 'obedience-then-grace' were the divine order, we would have to turn to techniques, systems and methods when we were hungry for God's will – and hope that our 'self-effort obedience' would be enough to attract God's attention and blessing.

But as God's will has priority in all things, and as his grace is infinite-and-absolute, we can turn to him when we hunger for his will *certain* that he is already calling us to him and to his promises.

Some believers suggest that the Father's willingness to speak to us is conditioned by our asking him to speak. They say that God is willing to speak, to give, to act, and so on, *when* we ask him. They imply that, generally, God does not speak to us unless we seek him.

But the biblical stress on grace means that our asking is conditioned by the Father's willingness. It is only because we know that it is God's will to speak to us that we dare ask him to speak.

We see this in Luke 11:13. This verse mentions the two important elements – *God's willingness* and *our asking* – and reveals God's way of acting, giving, speaking, and so on.

Luke 11:13 ☐

Some people think that the human asking in this verse comes before God's will, and is a pre-condition of his willingness to give the Spirit. But the scriptural 'grace first' emphasis means that our asking is the result and outworking of God's will to give his Spirit.

Believers who stress 'obedience first' concentrate on asking God to reveal his will – at the times of their choosing, when *they* want to know his will. Whereas those who emphasise 'grace first' focus on listening to God *all the time*, so that they do not miss those moments when *he* reveals his will to them.

We must constantly remember this basic principle of 'listening to God'. He does not speak to us just because *we* ask him to speak to us. Rather, we listen to him because *he* keeps on calling us to keep on listening to him. The priority and initiative is all with God.

UNDERSTANDING GOD'S WILL

We have noted that the primary purpose of listening to God is to know him better. God reveals his Word to us essentially to reveal himself to us. He speaks to us to draw us closer to him and deeper into him. True biblical listening always has a *relational* aim and foundation – guidance and doctrine are secondary.

In fact, we can say that the best way of understanding God's will is by getting to know God more intimately – hence our stress in this series on *Knowing the Father*, *Knowing the Son* and *Knowing the Spirit*.

Nevertheless, God does reveal his will to us when he speaks to us – though we must always appreciate the relational context and purpose of this revelation.

We have also seen that, because God is spiritual, he rarely reveals his Word with an audible voice which we hear with our physical ears. Instead he 'speaks' by the Spirit in a variety of ways which we are meant to 'hear' or 'discern' by faith in our *spirits*.

As well as breathing his Word to us through the Bible, God also communicates his will to our spirits in about ten other ways.

1.   Circumstances

Acts 16:6–10 □

We have seen, in Acts 16:6–10, that Paul was guided by the Spirit to God's particular will for his ministry to the Gentiles at that time. The passage does not make it clear how the Spirit prevented Paul from preaching in Asia or Bithynia: it may have been a supernatural check to his spirit, or it may have been a circumstantial difficulty. God uses both means, and neither is 'superior' to the other.

The New Testament shows that God guided Paul throughout his life by many means. From the events of Acts 21 onwards, however, Paul's circumstances appear to have been increasingly significant in helping Paul discern God's particular will for his life and ministry.

Circumstances do play a real part in helping us to understand God's will, but we must always look at them realistically – and then apply God's wisdom. We consider the whole area of 'judging' or 'testing' revelation in Part Eight.

Circumstances can be interpreted in different ways. For example:

- *God may use them to test our faith and perseverance*

- *the devil may use them to oppose us, and we may need to order them out of the way*

Some 'open doors' may lead to snares, while a few 'closed doors' may need to be forced open. This means that we should not be guided by circumstances alone, for that would be pagan fatalism; rather, we should ask God to give us the spiritual gift of his own wisdom or discernment so that we can interpret our circumstances correctly.

2.   Godly thinking

Romans 12:10 highlights the importance of a spiritually renewed mind, and shows its relevance to our understanding of God's will.

Romans 12:10 ☐

When God created humanity in his own image, he provided us with rational minds which he intended us to use; and Jesus reveals – in Matthew 22:37 – that we are to use *all* our minds to love God as intensely as possible. Furthermore, Philippians 2:5 teaches that believers can also be indwelt by the very mind of Jesus.

Matthew 22:37 ☐

Philippians 2:5 ☐

These three verses illustrate the importance of our minds. Despite this, at different times of history, some sections of the church have belittled the mind, and have devalued mental training and good education. But disciplined, developed thinking is central to Christian discipleship, for we cannot understand Jesus' parables and teaching if we do not use our minds.

The Holy Spirit does minister to our spirits, but he also comes to teach us and to lead us into all truth. This means that we need to respond to his work with both *mental effort* and *spiritual openness*.

God reveals his Word, his will, himself, to us as we use *every* faculty that he has given to us, and as we consider carefully our situation. As we see in Part Eight, we need to use our renewed minds to think everything through, to assess different factors, and to act wisely on the spiritual conclusions that we reach.

Much of the time, we do not need special 'supernatural' or 'circumstantial' guidance to understand God's will. Renewed thinking, godly common sense, are adequate for many things. Of course, we do all this in the light of God's Written Word and as the Holy Spirit empowers and renews our thinking to bring it more into line with God's way of thinking.

3.   The Spirit's witness

We know that God is a personal spiritual being who communicates with us through our spirits. He rarely 'speaks' to us with an audible voice which we 'hear' in our physical ears; instead, his Word and his will come to us on his breath, on his Spirit, and we 'hear' or 'discern' God's will by faith in our spirits.

When a man or woman is 'born again', they begin a new, personal 'Father/Child' relationship with God. The third person of God, the Holy Spirit, starts to 'witness' or 'communicate' with their spirits in a way which goes far beyond a rational, mental appreciation of facts, physical stimuli and biblical doctrines.

As we see in *Knowing the Spirit* and *Ministry in the Spirit*, the Holy Spirit speaks to us directly; he gives us an inner witness which is always fully aligned with the full truth of God's eternal Word.

It is difficult to describe the different ways that the Spirit gives this hidden witness, as he deals with each believer individually and distinctively. We can say, however, that he often provides his witness in one of three general ways. For example, he communicates:

• *through a mental or visual impression*

We may 'see' or 'feel' or 'hear' or 'sense' one of the Spirit's thoughts. We then have to judge whether our inner impression is due to human

Proverbs 20:27 ☐

Romans 8:16 ☐

imagination, demonic suggestion or divine revelation – we consider this in Part Eight. We can learn to recognise the Spirit's 'voice', much as we learn to recognise any unseen person's voice.

- *through an inner check*

We 'feel' or 'sense' an inner caution from the Spirit that something is not quite right. Of course, an uncomfortable feeling could be an unrecognised prejudice or it could have a straightforward physical explanation; but it may be the Spirit's way of checking our spirits and 'telling' us to hold on.

Again, we must 'test' or 'judge' this feeling before acting on it.

- *through an inner release*

We have an inner sense of peace or encouragement when faced with a choice or decision. We cannot explain this 'feeling' with our minds, but we sense in our spirits that God is at work and that the situation is somehow from him.

Such a feeling may be wishful thinking, human enthusiasm, natural optimism or godly encouragement. This means that we must learn to recognise the Spirit's way of communicating with us so that we can discern God's thoughts from human or demonic thoughts.

4.   A *rhema* word

We have seen that there are two Greek words for 'word'. *Logos* points to God's general word to all people, and *rhema* indicates his specific word to a particular person or group.

Romans 10:17 ☐

When the Spirit 'speaks' God's *rhema* word into our spirits, it is as if he uses a divine searchlight. By a *rhema* word, God pinpoints one aspect of his *general* Word from the Scriptures and reveals the 'now' Word which is supremely relevant to our situation. The Spirit takes this *rhema* Word, and communicates it personally and distinctively to us.

God's *rhema* word comes to us on God's *breath*, and it makes no difference whether we are listening to a sermon, reading the Bible, or in the middle of an everyday activity.

Whatever the circumstances, the Spirit makes us suddenly aware of a word, a sentence, a verse from the Bible, a line in a spiritual song, a thought, a 'message', and so on.

Each *rhema* word will always fully align with God's Personal Word, his Written Word, and with all other true *rhema* words. And it will highlight one particular aspect of God's general Word – that which is his 'now' word for us, in that particular situation, at that specific time.

5.   Godly desires

Psalm 37:4

Psalm 37:4 teaches a profound and liberating spiritual principle which suggests that God often reveals his will to us through our desires. If our deepest desire is godly, it may actually be God's will.

We must recognise that God's will is not always the opposite of what we want. As we live in God's presence, as we are increasingly controlled and directed by him, and as we are renewed by him in our thinking, so his desires 'naturally' become our desires. We find that we start to want what he wants.

Psalm 37:4, however, lays down a strict condition: we must delight in the Lord. This verse does not mean that we can continue in sin as long as we love God. For when we truly love God, we love what *he* loves and desire what *he* desires.

6.   Special guidance

Acts 16:6–10

There could be a distinction in Acts 16:6–10 between the general witness of the Spirit to Paul in verse 7, and the special supernatural guidance from the Spirit in verses 6 and 9.

Numbers 12:6

2 Kings 1:3–15

1 Chronicles 21:18

Isaiah 6

Ezekiel 12:8

Daniel 7:1

9:21

Zechariah 1:8–9

The Bible records several instances when God guides his servants through awesome and unusual means of guidance like visions and angelic visitations. We see this, for example, in Numbers 12:6; 2 Kings 1:3–15; 1 Chronicles 21:18; Isaiah 6; Ezekiel 12:8; Daniel 7:1; 9:21 and Zechariah 1:8–9.

We must recognise, however, that these are not God's usual way of communicating with us, and should not hanker after such experiences.

Acts 9:4–6

10:9–16

In his creative variety, God does, at times, 'speak' through amazing supernatural encounters like Acts 9:4–6 and 10:9–16, so we should not dismiss similar stories today. But they are not that common, so we must wonder about believers who suggest that God always speaks to them in these dramatic ways.

7.   The gifts of the Holy Spirit

In *Knowing the Spirit* and *Ministry in the Spirit*, we note that God has given special spiritual gifts of revelation to the church so that his will may be known – and we examine these gifts in some detail.

The gift of prophecy is especially relevant to 'listening to God', and we consider this in Parts Six and Seven.

All prophecy – both personal and congregational – must be 'weighed', 'judged', 'sifted' and 'tested'; and we examine this in Part Eight. Prophecy should never supersede the Written Word, or even contradict it. Where there is a discrepancy between a claimed prophecy and the Scriptures, the prophecy should be rejected.

At various times in church history, some Christian groups have become pre-occupied with personal prophecy – as though this were the definitive way that God communicated with his people. But personal prophecy is only one of the ways that God 'speaks', and it must be held alongside all the other ways that he uses to reveal his will.

1 Thessalonians 5:19–21 lays down the biblical balance: we must never treat any prophecy with contempt; but neither must we accept it without question. We must test everything, and hold on to only those parts of the prophecy which are good.

1 Thessalonians 5:19–21 ☐

As we see in Part Eight, we are under no spiritual obligation to follow a prophecy which does not 'witness' with our spirit. In general, personal and congregational prophecy should:

- *confirm what we sense that God is already 'saying'*

- *not be an attempt to manipulate or control a believer*

- *conform to both Scripture and renewed common sense*

We consider personal and congregational prophecy in Part Seven.

8.   The fruit of the Spirit

As we respond with 'gospel obedience' to any aspect of the ministry of the Holy Spirit, so he produces the distinctive 'fruit' in our lives which is described in Galatians 5:22. This means that, as we listen to the Spirit, so his guidance has the consequential effect of developing those character traits which indicate that he is at work in our lives.

Galatians 5:22 ☐

As a result, we can ask ourselves whether the guidance we think that we are receiving is producing – or is likely to produce – the fruit of the Spirit. Even when God is demolishing our human ideas and our old patterns of behaviour, there should be a deep and abiding sense of love, joy, peace, patience, and so on.

But the fruit of the Spirit is not merely the result of God's Word working in our lives, it is also one of God's ways of testing communications.

We have seen that a sense of 'inner peace' is part of the Spirit's witness to help us identify God's will. In fact, every aspect of the fruit of the Spirit is part of this inner witness. This means that, as the fruit develops in us, so we are better equipped to recognise God's voice and understand his will.

9.   Godly counsel

We consider the important ministry of counselling in *Ministry in the Spirit*, and the reality of this ministry – plus its high profile in the Bible – should be enough to convince us that God often reveals his will and purposes through committed, Spirit-anointed believers.

Proverbs 12:15 ☐
15:22 ☐

Passages like Proverbs 12:15 and 15:22 show that we should seek out godly and mature Christians – and listen to their advice. As with all the different means of guidance, we should listen to their advice but not accept it blindly. And, as with prophecy, we need to test it, to hold on to the part which is good – and then to act on the good and godly part.

Psalm 1:1–2 ☐

As disciples, we should be ready to submit our wills to whatever God says to us through counsellors and advisors. But we must remember Psalm 1:1–2, and take care that the advice we receive is biblical and is fully in line with the Word of God.

10.   The principle of agreement

Deuteronomy 19:15 ☐

2 Corinthians 13:1 ☐

God does not 'speak' to us in only one way, he always confirms his Word by revealing it in a variety of ways. Passages like Deuteronomy 19:15 and 2 Corinthians 13:1 reveal the eternal spiritual principle of *agreement* – which is founded in the nature of the triune God himself.

Every revelation is willed by the Father, spoken by the Word and carried out by the Spirit, but there is always perfect agreement between them. This is because, ultimately, there is only one revelation – and that is the self-revelation of God himself.

At different times, we may focus more on the will of the Father, or on the words of the Son, or on the actions of the Spirit; but we need to recognise that they all always agree with each other – they perfectly complement each other.

This means that we should not expect God to send two or three similar prophetic words to guide and direct us. Rather, we should expect him to reveal his Word to us in two or three different ways.

We must never assume that revelation will come to us from God in a particular form. He chooses how he speaks, and we listen to him according to his principles. In every situation, he chooses whether to speak to us through our circumstances, or through a dream, or through a sermon, or through a prophetic word, or through a verse – and then he confirms his revelation by revealing the same Word to us in other complementary ways.

God does not speak only through prophetic words, or only through visions, or only through circumstances, or only through a particular minister, and so on. We cannot know how God will speak to us, we can simply be certain that he is speaking to us.

This means that we should always be listening to God, always be fully alert for his Word and his will. Whenever we sense that he is guiding us, we should pray and wait for him to confirm his Word in other ways – without attempting to engineer something which will fit with *our* will.

It is wrong, however, to expect God to confirm something which he has already revealed in his Written Word, or to scan the Scriptures to find some obscure verse which we can use to confirm our sensing.

All guidance is subject to Scripture, not the other way around; but we must *listen* for God's voice, and not try to manipulate his Word.

PART FIVE

old testament prophetic listening

One of the themes of this *Sword of the Spirit* series is that all believers have an essentially 'prophetic' calling. As we see in *Knowing the Spirit* and *Ministry in the Spirit*, we are meant to be active partners with God rather than passive spectators of God: we are called to walk step-by-step with God, and to speak his words and do his deeds. It should be clear that this sort of partnership must be based on careful listening to God and an accurate understanding of his Word and will.

A good definition of general Christian prophecy is 'to hear or see what God is saying, and to pass it on'; and it is this broad understanding which reveals the general 'prophetic' calling of all believers. It also establishes the critical link between 'listening to God' and every form of Christian service or ministry.

Many modern believers concentrate on the 'speaking' element when they think about prophecy; but there can be no true prophetic speaking unless there has been real prophetic listening – and there can be no prophetic listening without a prophetic personal relationship with God.

THE PROPHETIC CALLING

In the Old Testament, most of the prophets were called a 'man of God'. This description suggests the intimate relationship which is at the heart of the prophetic calling.

Moses was the first prophet to be identified in this way; but he was followed by many others, for example, Deuteronomy 33:1; 1 Samuel 2:27; 9:6; 1 Kings 13; 20:28; 25:7–9; 2 Kings 4:7; 2 Chronicles 25:7–9 and Nehemiah 12:24.

The Old Testament prophets were also often called 'servants'. Although the phrase 'the servant of God' is given only to Moses, 'his' 'your' and 'my' servant are used of most other prophets. 2 Kings 17:13 and Ezra 9:11 illustrate the close servant relationship that Old Testament prophets enjoyed with God.

Three Hebrew words are translated in the Old Testament as 'prophet'. They all seem to be used synonymously.

- *Nabi* suggests the idea of 'calling'. It shows that prophets are 'called by God' and are 'called to God' – so that they can 'call to God' and can 'call for God'.

- *Roeh* and *hozeh* both suggest the idea of 'seeing'. They show that prophets 'see God', 'see what God is doing', 'see human events from God's perspective' and 'are seen by men and women'.

These Hebrew words convey the essence of the prophetic calling – which is to be called by God, to see and hear those things which remain invisible and inaudible to other people, and to call to people for God.

The purpose of the prophetic calling

We have seen that God 'speaks' his Word essentially to reveal *himself*; we should therefore expect that an intimate personal knowledge of God will be at the heart of the prophetic calling. God always reveals himself, and 'speaks' to us, so that we might know *him* – and so that we might fulfil our main purpose as men and women in this life.

In the Bible, Abraham is the first person to be identified as a prophet, and we can trace the development of the intimate personal 'knowing' relationship which led to his prophetic ministry.

- *Acts 7:1–2* reports how God first appeared to Abraham and spoke to him

- *Isaiah 41:8* shows that Abraham then became God's friend

- *Genesis 18:17–21* describes how God went on to reveal his intentions to his friend

The twin principles that prophetic revelation is essentially for the knowledge of God, and that this revelation is given mainly in the context of intimate relationship, can be seen, for example, in 1 Samuel 3:7; Isaiah 50:4–5; Amos 3:7; Daniel 9:23; 10:11 and John 13:21–26.

This suggests that our prophetic calling is primarily a summons to an intimate relationship with God. He then reveals the secrets of his hearts – his burdens, joys, desires, intentions and instructions – to those people who have obeyed his summons and are listening particularly intently.

The calling

Old Testament prophets could not call themselves to God; they had to be called, or summoned, by God. As ever, the initiative is clearly with God alone.

All the different biblical accounts of prophetic calling reveal the inherent power of God's call. The people summoned to God either had to set aside what they were doing and begin listening to God, or they had to disobey God's Word and will.

We see this, for example, in Exodus 3:1–10; 1 Samuel 3:1–21; 1 Kings 19:16, 19–21; 2 Kings 2:9–15; Isaiah 6:1–9; Jeremiah 1:4–10; Ezekiel 1; 2:3; Hosea 1:2; Amos 7:14–15 and Jonah 1:1.

The primary object of the Old Testament prophetic calling was to summon the man or woman into the presence of the holy God – and only secondarily to send them on a divine errand.

Only when the person had stood before God, and had listened to his Word, could they stand before men and women in the world. We see this particularly clearly in the life of the Moses: for example, Exodus 3:4–10; 33:11; 34:34–35; Numbers 12:1–8; Deuteronomy 5:4; 34:10.

When prophets obeyed the call and entered into the presence of God, their function was simply to listen to him as he whispered his secrets. As we have noted, God never does anything without first revealing his

Acts 7:1–2 ☐

Isaiah 41:8 ☐

Genesis
       18:17–21 ☐

1 Samuel 3:7 ☐

Isaiah 50:4–5 ☐

Amos 3:7 ☐

Daniel 9:23 ☐
       10:11 ☐

John 13:21–26 ☐

Exodus 3:1–10 ☐

1 Samuel 3:1–21 ☐

1 Kings
       19:16–21 ☐

2 Kings 2:9–15 ☐

Isaiah 6:1–9 ☐

Jeremiah 1:4–10 ☐

Ezekiel 1 ☐
       2:3 ☐

Hosea 1:2 ☐

Amos 7:14–15 ☐

Jonah 1:1 ☐

Exodus 3:4–10 ☐
       33:11 ☐
       34:34–35 ☐

Numbers 12:1–8 ☐

Deuteronomy
       5:4 ☐
       34:10 ☐

intention to his servants the prophets. This should help us to appreciate the great importance of listening within our partnership with God.

Having faced God, and having heard his Word and his *particular* will, the prophets were then sent to specific situations with a specific message. We can see this in 1 Kings 22; Jeremiah 23:22 & Amos 3:7.

THE PROPHETIC FUNCTION

After listening, the main function of Old Testament prophets was to speak *God's* words. They had to act on what they had heard. We see this in Exodus 3:14; 4:13–17; 6:28 – 7:2; Jeremiah 1:9 & Isaiah 6:6–7.

1.   To speak God's words

The main thrust of the prophetic message was always 'get right with God'. The prophets gave warnings about the future which they validated by quoting examples of God's dealings in the past. They called the ungodly to repentance by painting a picture of the wrath to come. They declared the anger of God against individuals and nations, and attempted to introduce a healthy fear of God into each situation.

As far as the Old Testament prophets were concerned, reconciliation with God was only possible when people were aware of God's holy wrath and had a right attitude towards him. These 'reconciliation' prophecies form the bulk of Old Testament prophecy. Amos 5; Zephaniah 1:14–2:3 and Hosea 5 are typical of this sort of prophecy.

Occasionally, the prophets spoke in terms of future blessing and called the godly to greater holiness – as in Isaiah 2:2–5. They charged God's people with living according to their calling. This is just a different way of expressing the same 'get right with God' message.

2.   To reveal God's compassion

Moses was the supreme prophet of the Old Testament, and his divinely inspired emphasis on moral and social justice runs through the Jewish Law, for example, Leviticus 19:9–18 and Deuteronomy 23:15–25.

God's compassion was underlined by the later prophets: we see this, for example, in 2 Chronicles 28:9–15 and Amos 2:6–7; 4:1–3; 8:4–8.

3. To provide God's insight

The prophets were often called seers – 'see-ers' – in Israel because they provided the people with God's insight into both the future and contemporary events: we see this, for example, in Deuteronomy 18:22 and Isaiah 1:7–9.

They constantly reminded the people of what God had done; and they used this understanding of the past to reveal God's nature. Based on this, they would then reveal what God was about to do. This was not inspired guesswork; it was divine revelation. They did not make projections; they prophesied: that is, they spoke what they had heard God say to them while they were listening to him, and what they knew of his unchanging character through their relationship with him.

In particular, the prophets called people away from false gods to the one true God. They did this by reminding the people how God had dealt in the past with those who had departed from the sole worship of *Yahweh*. We can see this in Isaiah 41:21–23 & 45:20–22.

At times, the prophets announced events which were about to take place in the near future, and, in the same breath, with the same words, predicted another event which was, maybe, a thousand years away.

In Deuteronomy 18:15, Moses reassured the people about what would happen when he died. He had Joshua in mind as the prophet 'from among yourselves'. But this was *also* a prediction about another 'Yeshua' from Nazareth some 1500 years later. Isaiah 7:14 is another example of this type of 'insight' – or 'now and then' – prophecy.

Some prophets played a leading role in national events, and the first two kings, Saul and David, were also prophets. From then on, there was a close link between the anointed king and the anointed prophet.

Sometimes, a king would consult a prophet to learn God's thoughts or to take divine advice – as in 1 Kings 14:1–18; 2 Kings 6:21–23; 8:7–8; 2 Chronicles 34:22–28. At other times, a prophet was sent to confront a ruler with a message from God – for example, 1 Kings 11:29–39; 13:1–10; 18:1–2. This reminds us that God 'speaks' about every aspect of life, and not just about the 'spiritual' elements.

2 Chronicles 28:9–15	☐
Amos 2:6–7	☐
4:1–3	☐
8:4–8	☐
Deuteronomy 18:22	☐
Isaiah 1:7–9	☐
Isaiah 41:21–23	☐
45:20–22	☐
Deuteronomy 18:15	☐
Isaiah 7:14	☐
1 Kings 14:1–18	☐
2 Kings 6:21–23	☐
8:7–8	☐
2 Chronicles 34:22–28	☐
1 Kings 11:29–39	☐
13:1–10	☐
18:1–2	☐

4.   To announce God's deeds

God's servants the prophets are the only people that the Old Testament records as being involved with the miraculous – with signs, wonders and healings: these are a frequent part of the prophetic ministry.

Only those men and women who have been anointed with God's Spirit are able to be 'do-ers' of God's deeds. We see this, for example, in Genesis 20; Numbers 12; 1 Kings 13; 17:7–24; 2 Kings 4:8–37; 20:1–11; 2 Chronicles 25:5–16 & Jeremiah 38:14–28.

As we note in *Ministry in the Spirit*, this is a partnership with God and not a personal capacity to work miracles. Our special responsibility is to listen to God – and then to speak his words and follow his instructions. God works the miracle; prophets merely announce what they have heard God 'say' in the privacy of their intimate relationship.

5.   To intercede with God

Genesis 20:7 describes Abraham, the first prophet, as being able to plead successfully with God – and so to bring change to the situation. Intercession is central to the prophetic calling, for prophets are those who call to God and are called into God's presence for consultation.

Exodus 18:19 records Jethro's suggestion that Moses should make intercession his priority, and Numbers 27:5 shows that Moses implemented this advice.

Time and again, the Old Testament prophets became known as such effective intercessors that kings would beg them to plead with God on their behalf. We see this, for example, in 1 Kings 13:6; 2 Kings 19:4 & Zechariah 7:1–3.

PROPHETIC INSPIRATION

It should be plain that the prophets had to be inspired by God to function prophetically. They needed to listen carefully for his insight and instructions: prophetic listening *always* preceded prophetic speaking and prophetic actions.

The Old Testament records that the prophets were guided or inspired mainly by either 'the Word of God' or 'the Spirit of God'.

We can say that some prophets, for example, Moses, were principally 'Word inspired' prophets; and that others, like Elijah, were mainly 'Spirit inspired' prophets. But this should not be over-emphasised.

The Word of the Lord

The Old Testament suggests that the Word of the Lord had a dynamic impact on the prophets: this is very clear in Amos 3:8. The Scriptures often use the phrase, 'the Word of the Lord came to'; and this underlines both the living nature of the Word and the divine initiative.

Amos 3:8 ☐

'Came to' is better translated as either 'became actively present to'; or, more simply, as 'was to'. In Zechariah 1:1, the 'coming' of God's Word seems to take much of the eighth month; whereas, in Zechariah 1:7, the Word comes on the twenty fourth day of the eleventh month. This suggests that the coming of God's Word can refer to an inner awareness of God's particular message which develops over time, as well as to a more immediate awareness of God's voice.

Zechariah 1:1–7 ☐

Because God's Word, like God, is infinite, eternal and always with us, the coming of his Word can highlight a truth which is already known or it can reveal something which had been previously unknown.

God's Word sometimes came to the prophets in a dramatic supernatural experience – as in Isaiah 6:1–10 and Ezekiel 1:1–3. But at other times it came in the context of ordinary events like the sight of an almond tree, two baskets of figs, and visits to a workshop and building site – as in Jeremiah 1:11; 18:1–4; 24 and Amos 7:7.

Isaiah 6:1–10 ☐

Ezekiel 1:1–3 ☐

Jeremiah 1:11 ☐

18:1–4 ☐

18:24 ☐

These incidents show that God 'spoke' his Word to his listening servants in the intimacy of private fellowship and their everyday lives, and in ordinary terms that they understood and could easily pass on.

Amos 7:7 ☐

The burden of the Lord

Habakkuk 1:1 refers to God's *massa*. Some translations render this as 'message' or 'oracle', but it literally means a heavy load or burden. It suggests the idea of God allowing a prophet to feel the weight or intensity of his feelings about a particular matter.

Habakkuk 1:1 ☐

Isaiah often felt the burden of the Lord about other nations – as in Isaiah 13–23; and Jeremiah 23:33–40 identifies false prophets as a particular burden of the Lord. Again, this appears to be a growing awareness in the prophet's spirit which develops through intimate fellowship and careful listening.

The Spirit of the Lord

The Old Testament presents a very strong link between the Spirit and prophecy. We see this, for example, in Numbers 11:29; 1 Samuel 10; 19:18–24; Micah 3:8 and Joel 2:28.

It is clear that, in the Old Testament, the anointing of the Spirit usually resulted in the activity of divine prophesying. This appears to refer to a more instant type of inspiration for immediate proclamation.

Dreams, visions and angels

The Old Testament prophets were often inspired through visions by day and dreams by night. We see this, for example, in Numbers 12:6; Isaiah 6; Ezekiel 12:8; Daniel 7:1 and Zechariah 1:8.

In contrast, the Bible mentions few examples of angels being sent to prophets: 2 Kings 1:3–15, 1 Chronicles 21:18, Daniel 9:21 and Zechariah 1:9 are the only recorded incidents.

This may be because the prophetic calling is based on an intimate, face-to-face relationship with God himself; or it may be because, as God's messengers, angels and prophets have a very similar function.

PROPHETIC MINISTRY

Although all the Old Testament prophets were inspired by the same God, by *Yahweh*, they each had a different and distinctive style of ministering. Isaiah, for example, is as different from Ezekiel as Rembrandt is from Picasso. The words were God's, but they were also human: prophetic ministry is a genuine partnership between a master and a servant – who happen to be very close friends.

Prophetic words

The Old Testament prophets knew that they were only God's mouthpieces: they were merely passing on the revelation that they had received through their prophetic listening.

But divine inspiration is not the same as divine dictation. The prophets always received the *rhema* 'essence' directly from God, but they coloured and flavoured that 'essence' with their own personalities, backgrounds and culture.

They then spoke the 'coloured and flavoured Word' in a wide variety of human styles. No one means of communication was always right, they used whichever style was most appropriate for the particular people that they were addressing.

In the Old Testament, we see the prophets using, for example, narrative verse, prose, parables, direct speech, satire, psalms, laments, preaching, and so on.

Whatever form their words took, the prophets never expressed a human opinion when they spoke. Instead, they brought an utterance which altered the situation – what they announced always occurred.

Isaiah 40:6–8 and Isaiah 55:11 reveal the awesome power of the prophetic spoken word, and we consider this throughout *Ministry in the Spirit*.

Isaiah 40:6–8 ☐
55:11 ☐

Prophetic lives

As we have noted, the prophet calling is not essentially to function as a divine mouthpiece; rather, it is primarily to live in an intimate 'known and knowing' relationship with the holy God. This means that the prophets' lives were as important as their words in revealing God.

The Scriptures make it clear that Hosea's unhappy marriage was a potent symbol, Jeremiah's life was an uncompromising lesson, Ezekiel was a sign to the house of Israel, and Isaiah and his children were signs and portents.

The way that the prophets lived proclaimed a message of God's justice and reconciliation which was just as powerful as their words: they were not 'men of God' for nothing. We see this, for example, in Isaiah 8:18; Jeremiah 16; Ezekiel 4:3; 12:6; 24:24 and Hosea 1:3.

Isaiah 8:18 ☐
Jeremiah 16 ☐
Ezekiel 4:3 ☐
12:6 ☐
24:24 ☐
Hosea 1:3 ☐

Prophetic actions

Some Old Testament prophets used symbolic, dramatic actions as part of their way of communicating God's Word to the people around them – for example, Exodus 17:9; Jeremiah 19:1, 10, 11; Ezekiel 4:1–3.

These were not 'visual aids'; they were prophetic deeds which, in their own right, proclaimed what the prophets had heard God speak.

As we have noted, many prophetic actions were supernatural signs and wonders. In fact, the Old Testament only describes anointed prophets acting as God's partners in miracles and healings. The lives of Moses, Elijah and Elisha contain many famous examples, but 1 Kings 13:1–10 shows that God also used other prophets.

FALSE PROPHECY

It is important to grasp that the Bible does not lay down a test for establishing a false prophecy. Instead, it provides a series of principles by which false prophets can be distinguished from true prophets.

This suggests that we should concentrate more on the foundation of prophecy – the listening intimate relationship with God – than on the prophetic words and deeds.

We consider the issues of false prophets and judging revelation in Part Eight. But, for now, we can note that Moses offers two tests in Deuteronomy 13:1–5 and Deuteronomy 18:21–22.

Moses teaches that false prophets can be identified by:

- *the failure of their predictive prophecies (but the corollary is not necessarily true, fulfilment is not a proof of genuineness)*

- *the way they call people after gods other than the one true God*

Jeremiah 23:9–40 and Ezekiel 12:21–14:11 offer three further tests.

- *their lifestyles are immoral*

- *they do not check immorality in others*

- *they call for peace with no regard to the moral and spiritual conditions required for peace*

Sidebar references:

Exodus 17:9 ☐

Jeremiah 19:1 ☐
　　　19:10–11 ☐

Ezekiel 4:1–3 ☐

1 Kings 13:1–10 ☐

Deuteronomy
　　　13:1–5 ☐
　　　18:21–22 ☐

Jeremiah
　　　23:9–40 ☐

Ezekiel 12:21–
　　　14:11 ☐

We establish in *Ministry in the Spirit* that genuine Old Testament prophecy is the essential foundation upon which any understanding of contemporary ministry must be built. Now we can appreciate that prophetic listening is absolutely fundamental to all biblical prophesying – and so to every aspect of the Christian life.

As, through this book, we develop our understanding of the 'God speaking/ believers listening' process, we will often return to this Old Testament prophetic foundation.

We do not listen to God to enjoy a pleasant sound; rather, we listen to him so that we can be drawn deeper into his life – and can then be sent out with his Word to the church and the world.

PART SIX

new testament prophetic listening

We have seen, in Deuteronomy 18:14–20, that Moses prophetically prepared the people of Israel for the leadership of Joshua, and – *with the same words* – also prophetically announced that God would, one day, send another prophet who would be like himself.

By the time of Jesus, the Jews expected that their coming *Messiah* would be a second Moses – that he would be another prophet to whom God would reveal himself as intimately as in Numbers 12:6–8; another servant who would repeat, on a grand scale, the miraculous deeds of the Exodus.

When the priests and levites questioned John the Baptist, in John 1:19–25, they were eager to establish whether John was 'the Prophet' – the one who had been prophesied by Moses in Deuteronomy 18:15–20. While, in Acts 3:22–24, Peter shows he believed that Jesus was this long-awaited supreme prophet.

Even though most people at that time did not believe that Jesus was divine, and only a few realised that he was the *Messiah*, many Jews

Deuteronomy 18:15–20 ☐

Numbers 12:6–8 ☐

John 1:19–25 ☐

Acts 3:22–24 ☐

recognised that Jesus was 'a' prophet – if not 'the' prophet. For
example, we see:

Luke 24:19 ☐

- *Cleopas realised that Jesus was a prophet because of the things he
  said and did* – Luke 24:19

John 4:18 ☐

- *the Samaritan woman at Jacob's well understood that Jesus
  was a prophet when the Spirit told him about her husbands* – John
  4:18

John 6:14 ☐

- *the crowds received Jesus as a prophet when he fed the five
  thousand* – John 6:14

Matthew 21:11 ☐

- *they also received him as a prophet when he rode into Jerusalem on
  the donkey* – Matthew 21:11

John 7:52 ☐

- *Christ's enemies referred to him as a prophet in the dispute with
  Nicodemus* – John 7:52

Matthew 13:57 ☐

- *Jesus seemed to consider himself to be a prophet* – Matthew 13:57

JESUS 'THE' PROPHET

Numbers 12:6–8 ☐
Deuteronomy
         18:14–17 ☐
Isaiah 42:1–9 ☐
         49:1–7 ☐
         50:4–11 ☐
         52:13–
         53:12 ☐

Jesus was both 'the' great Prophet of Numbers 12:6–8 & Deuteronomy 18:14–17 and 'the' prophetic Suffering Servant of God who
perfectly fulfilled the four prophetic songs of Isaiah 42:1–9; 49:1–7;
50:4–11 and 52:13–53:12.

We can say that, throughout his earthly life and ministry,
Jesus manifested all the signs of an extraordinary prophet. For
example:

He knew God

John 1:18 ☐

The Old Testament prophets were close to God's heart, but John 1:18
shows that Jesus was nearest of all to the Father's heart.

Matthew 11:27 ☐

The prophets shared God's secrets, yet Matthew 11:27 suggests a
degree of intimacy which was even greater than Moses'. The prophets
knew God and revealed him through their lives, words and deeds; but
only Jesus knew and revealed the Father perfectly.

We know that Jesus is the Son of God, the Lamb of God, the Personal Word of God, the Light of the World, and so on; as such, he is the great and perfect prophetic revealer of God the Father. We consider this more fully in *Knowing the Father* and *Knowing the Son*.

John 1:8 ☐
1:18 ☐
1:36 ☐
8:12 ☐
8:17–26 ☐
8:38 ☐

He listened and obeyed

Even though John's Gospel gives a much greater emphasis to Jesus' divinity than the other three Gospels, it is also the Gospel which most stresses the fact that Jesus is totally under his Father's authority. It makes it plain that Jesus never goes anywhere, does anything, speaks or acts except in obedient response to an initiative from his Father.

We see this, for example, in John 4:34; 5:19, 30; 6:38; 7:28–29; 8:28–29; 10:18 and 12:49–50.

John 4:34 ☐
5:19 ☐
5:30 ☐
6:38 ☐
7:28–29 ☐
8:28–29 ☐
10:18 ☐
12:49–50 ☐

This means that prophetic listening and gospel obedience are fundamental to Jesus' life and ministry. He is the 'sent' one who, like the Old Testament prophets, responds obediently both to his summons to God and to the prophetic commission which he hears in his spirit during his listening. He listens, obeys, and acts on what he hears.

Matthew 15:24 shows that Jesus was sent to a clearly delineated area with a unique prophetic calling. He was to prophesy to a certain people, in a particular place, for a limited period of time.

Matthew 15:24 ☐

The sudden appearance and commencement of prophetic activity – which we see, for example, in Elijah and Amos – is repeated in Jesus' life. One day he was a carpenter whom nobody appears to have noticed as being unusual. Then he was called, publicly anointed, and sent.

Just six weeks later, Jesus was healing the sick, casting out demons, healing the sick and speaking God's powerful words – with an authority which astonished those who encountered him.

He spoke God's words

We have noted that prophets are God's mouthpiece; they announce *his* thoughts and insights, not their own. John 12:49–50 and 14:10 shows that Jesus claimed no originality for his speech: every word that he spoke was what the Father had told him. His prophetic words were based entirely on his prophetic listening.

John 12:49–50 ☐
14:10 ☐

He performed God's deeds

But Jesus was not all talk and no action. He was the Prophet 'mighty in word *and* deed'. Like so many of his prophetic forebears, his words were confirmed by his deeds.

At different times in church history, some believers have so stressed and defended the divinity of Jesus that they have almost dehumanised him – when we know that he was both fully God *and* fully human.

But an over-emphasis on Jesus' divinity can give the impression that Jesus healed the sick and worked miracles *because* he was God. If this were true, however, it would cast doubts on Jesus' promises to his followers of 'greater things' and 'signs following'.

The servant prophets of the Old Testament partnered God in healing the sick, raising the dead and working wonders because they had been anointed with the Spirit of God, and because they listened intently to God and followed his instructions with great care.

John 9:17 ☐ In the same way, Jesus performed God's deeds because he was a humble, serving human who was full of the Spirit of God, who listened to his Father, and who limited his words and actions to his divine instructions. In John 9:17, a blind beggar identified Jesus as a prophet precisely because he had opened his eyes: for him, the miracle was an evidence of Jesus' prophetic calling; it did not suggest divinity.

As we note in *Ministry in the Spirit*, this important truth means that the miraculous is accessible to every believer who has been anointed with the Spirit, who keeps on listening carefully to God and responding to him with gospel obedience.

Acts 10:34–48 ☐

Isaiah 61:1 ☐ The link in the Old Testament between the Spirit and prophecy is brought to a climax in Jesus' life. Acts 10:34–48 records Peter's address at the house of Cornelius. By quoting Isaiah 61:1 and applying it to Jesus, Peter makes it clear that it is Jesus' public anointing with the Spirit which makes the difference.

Matthew 3:16–17 ☐ Jesus' baptism was a pivotal moment in his life. As he rose from the river Jordan, in Matthew 3:16–17, the Spirit came down upon him. Of course, Jesus had been the *Christos*, the *Messiah*, the 'Anointed' throughout all eternity; but, in that moment of public anointing, the Son of God was set apart as a beloved Spirit-anointed prophet – with a special summons to intimacy with the Father, and with a unique commission of serving words and sacrificial work.

He anointed others

The Old Testament records that some prophets revealed those whom God had chosen to serve as kings or prophets, and then anointed them for service. We see this, for example, in 1 Kings 19:15–16.

1 Kings 19:15–16 ☐

This pattern continues in the New Testament, and John the Baptist prophetically introduced Jesus as the one who would baptise, or anoint, people in the Spirit. This is such a vital truth that it is the only incident which is described in all four Gospels and Acts – Matthew 3:1–12; Mark 1:1–8; Luke 3:1–18; John 1:19–34 & Acts 1:1–5.

Matthew 3:1–12 ☐
Mark 1:1–8 ☐
Luke 3:1–18 ☐
John 1:19–34 ☐
Acts 1:1–5 ☐

When Jesus returned to heaven, his first prophetic activity was to anoint his bride with the Holy Spirit, to commission and equip the church as a race of prophets, to summon his people to intimate listening, and to send us out as his prophetic, serving partners. We consider this in *Knowing the Spirit* and *Ministry in the Spirit*.

He interceded with God

Jesus second post-ascension prophetic action was to intercede at the Father's right hand. We see this in Romans 8:34 and Hebrews 7:25.

Romans 8:34 ☐
Hebrews 7:25 ☐

We have noted that the prophets were the intercessors of the Old Testament, and Jesus' life was also filled with listening prayer and intercession. The Gospels record, for example, that Jesus prayed:

- *early in the morning* – Mark 1:35

Mark 1:35 ☐

- *late in the evening* – Luke 6:12

Luke 6:12 ☐

- *at his baptism* – Luke 3:21

Luke 3:21 ☐

- *after much ministry* – Mark 1:35, 6:46, Luke 5:16

Mark 1:35 ☐
6:46 ☐
Luke 5:16 ☐

- *for a night before selecting the twelve disciples* – Luke 6:12

Luke 6:12 ☐

- *alone in the presence of his disciples* – Luke 9:18

9:18 ☐

- *at his transfiguration* – Luke 9:28–29

9:28–29 ☐

- *after the last supper* – John 17

John 17 ☐

- *in Gethsemane* – Mark 14:32, Luke 22:41

Mark 14:32 ☐
Luke 22:41 ☐

- *for Peter* – Luke 22:32

22:32 ☐

- *for small children* – Matthew 19:13–15

Matthew 19:13–15 ☐

Luke 23:34 ☐
    24:30 ☐
    24:50 ☐

John 14:16 ☐

- *at his crucifixion* – Luke 23:34

- *after his resurrection* – Luke 24:30

- *at his ascension* – Luke 24:50

- *after his ascension* – John 14:16

Jesus' prophetic intercession is particularly plain in John 17. Here he prays for himself, for the eleven disciples, and for us. We consider this more fully in *Effective Prayer*.

He was committed to truth, justice and God's compassion

John 14:6 ☐

Matthew 15:32 ☐
    20:34 ☐

Luke 7:13 ☐
    10:33 ☐

John 8:1–12 ☐

Jesus was totally committed to God's truth, and John 14:6 shows that he was the living embodiment of that truth. Throughout his life, Jesus was characterised and motivated by God's compassion – we see this, for example, in Matthew 15:32; 20:34; Luke 7:13 & 10:33.

Passages like John 8:1–12 and Matthew 23:23 suggest that truth which is empty of compassion is not God's truth. The whole of the Sermon on the Mount, Matthew 5–7, is Jesus' exposition of God's compassionate, truthful way of living. We consider this throughout *The Rule of God*, where we see how Jesus' personal rule more than fulfils the Old Testament prophets' inspired instructions.

He provided divine insight

Matthew
    26:64–68 ☐

Psalm 110 ☐

Daniel 7:13 ☐

Jesus followed in the footsteps of his prophetic forebears in every possible way. He was even crucified as a false prophet: in Matthew 26:64–68, Jesus acknowledged that he was the Messiah, and then revealed himself as the Lord of Psalm 110 and the mysterious heavenly person of Daniel 7:13. The Sanhedrin's response to these bold claims was to label Jesus as a false prophet and to call for his death.

Matthew
    11:20–24 ☐

John 21:15–19 ☐

Luke 21:20–24 ☐

Jesus was even a true prophet in the way that he provided God's insights into local situations and individual lives. We see this, for example, in Matthew 11:20–24 and John 21:15–19.

He also spoke predictively, in exactly the same manner as the Old Testament prophets. Jesus' words in Luke 21:20–24 were spoken in about AD 33. Approximately thirty-seven years later, in AD 70, Titus' Roman army surrounded Jerusalem, and the Christian community remembered this prophecy. They evacuated the city and were guided to Pella: contemporary records indicate that no believers were captured or killed in the ensuing massacre. The accuracy of this prophecy should assure us that Jesus' other prophecy in Luke 21:25–28 will also be fulfilled.

Luke 21:25–28 ☐

More than a prophet

Most false religions acknowledge that Jesus is a prophet. And it may be that their admission is the reason why some sections of the church give so little attention to Jesus' prophetic calling and activity.

Yet Jesus was much more than just another prophet. His birth, life, ministry, death, resurrection, ascension and anointing activity at Pentecost confirmed all that the Old Testament prophets had foretold. And Acts 10:43 identifies Jesus as the one to whom all other prophets bear witness. In fact, over three hundred detailed prophecies in the Old Testament were fulfilled in his life.

Acts 10:43 ☐

A prophet can do no more than speak or demonstrate the Word of God, but Jesus was the Word incarnate; and Revelation 19:10 teaches that all prophecy should be operated by the Spirit of Jesus *and* must bear testimony to him. This shows both that Jesus is the supreme prophet, and that all others who prophesy must point to him.

Revelation 19:10 ☐

We can say that Jesus is:

- *our example in prophesying*

- *the source of our prophesying*

- *the object of our prophesying.*

PROPHECY IN THE EARLY CHURCH

Jesus' anointing, or baptising activity, at Pentecost inaugurated a new prophetic era. The basic Old Testament understanding of prophecy was retained; but the church, instead of isolated individuals, became the centre of prophetic activity – and prophetic listening and living became central to the church.

The book of Acts records how the risen Christ directed the early church through prophetic revelation and insights. We see, for example:

- *Acts 5:1–11* – Peter prophetically exposed Ananias and Sapphira's and announced God's judgement

- *Acts 8:20–24* – Peter prophetically revealed Simon's inner thoughts and motivation

- *Acts 9:10–19* – Ananias received prophetic revelation about Paul's conversion and future ministry

- *Acts 10:1–19* – Cornelius and Peter received prophetic visions which guided them and led to the conversion of Cornelius' household

- *Acts 11:27–30* – Agabus prophetically predicted a famine in Judea

- *Acts 13:1–4* – Paul and Barnabas were sent on a missionary journey through a prophetic confirmation and revelation of God's will

- *Acts 13:9–12* – Paul prophetically announced God's judgement on Elymas when he was preventing the proconsul from coming to faith in Christ

- *Acts 14:9* – Paul received the prophetic insight that the lame man had faith to be healed

- *Acts 15:13–19* – James spoke a prophetic word of wisdom at the Jerusalem meeting considering the issue of Gentile believers

- *Acts 15:32* – Judas and Silas exercised a prophetic ministry of strengthening and encouragement at Antioch

- *Acts 16:6–7* – Paul's second missionary journey was prophetically directed by the Spirit

- *Acts 16:9–10* – Paul was prophetically directed by a vision to preach the gospel in Europe

- *Acts 21:9* – Philip had four daughters who prophesied

- *Acts 21:10–11* – Agabus prophetically predicted what would happen to Paul

- *Acts 27:23–26* – Paul received prophetic revelation about the shipwreck

Acts 5:1–11 ☐

8:20–24 ☐

9:10–19 ☐

10:1–19 ☐

11:27–30 ☐

13:1–4 ☐

13:9–12 ☐

14:9 ☐

15:13–19 ☐

15:32 ☐

16:6–7 ☐

16:9–10 ☐

21:9 ☐

21:10–11 ☐

27:23–26 ☐

Revelation 11:3–13 shows that prophecy and prophetic witness are among God's priorities in the last days – they did not cease with the early church and the book of Acts.

Revelation 11:3–13 ☐

The two lamps appear to refer to Moses and Elijah, the witnesses of Jesus' transfiguration. As we have seen, they are the supreme Old Testament examples of 'Word' and 'Spirit' inspired prophecy, and this passage shows that both these aspects of prophecy continue after Pentecost, and on to the end of this age.

The two olive trees seem to symbolise Joshua and Zerubbabel in Zechariah 3–4. They were the spiritual and civil leaders of the repatriated community who restored Jerusalem and the Temple after the Exile. This suggests that prophecy should still be directed to both the spiritual and the secular areas of life, and not just to the church.

Zechariah 3–4 ☐

Joshua and Zerubbabel were the two leaders who built the new Temple, and nothing builds the church like prophetic listening and living. In teaching that prophets are part of the foundation of the church, Ephesians 2:20 prefigures Revelation 11.

Ephesians 2:20 ☐

A prophetic people

Numbers 11:16–30 records how Moses' prophetic burden could be shared only with those who received the Spirit. When Joshua queried Eldad and Medad's prophesying, Moses answered him with an important prophetic prayer.

Numbers 11:16–30 ☐

God heard this prayer, and Joel 2:28–29 foretold his answer. God kept his promise at Pentecost, when Jesus poured the Spirit *without restriction* upon the church.

Joel 2:28–29 ☐

When Peter quoted this Joel prophecy, in Acts 2:18, he was inspired to add the important phrase, 'and they shall prophesy'. This shows that, since Pentecost, the possibility of prophetic listening, prophetic speaking and prophetic actions has been open to every believer who has been anointed with the Holy Spirit.

Acts 2:18 ☐

As we see in *Knowing the Spirit*, there was no limitation on the giving of the Spirit on the day of Pentecost, and no restriction on the receiving. Potentially, every believer – with no distinction between male and female, old and young, educated and illiterate – can prophesy.

When Peter mentioned prophecy in Acts 2:18, he surely meant that the whole church would minister like the Old Testament prophets.

This means that – as a result of the Spirit's outpouring at Pentecost – the whole people of God can be 'men of God', 'servants of God', 'called and calling', 'seen and seeing'.

All redeemed and anointed believers can, for example, now:

- *enter into the presence of God*

- *listen to God's secrets*

- *pass on God's thoughts about reconciliation, justice and events*

- *predict and proclaim*

- *intercede*

- *be inspired by the 'Word' and the 'Spirit'*

- *receive dreams and visions*

- *listen, speak, live and share in the miraculous*

It is important, however, to recognise that Peter's promise was not that all believers could be prophets, but that all could prophesy. There is a significant difference.

The prophesying of the early church is seen in the everyday behaviour of ordinary believers in the book of Acts; but there still remained a few individuals who were called prophets.

As we see in *Ministry in the Spirit*, it is the same in other areas of ministry. All are commissioned to evangelise, but not all are evangelists; all are commanded to heal; but not all are healers; all are called to teach, but not all are teachers – and so on.

Prophetic witness

The New Testament stresses that prophecy is part of the whole witness of the church. *Marturia*, 'witness' is the general term for the church's 'outreach' activity; and *kerugma*, 'preaching', and *propheteia*, 'prophecy' are aspects of this witnessing.

Revelation 19:10 □

Revelation 19:10 develops this. It does not state that all prophecy should be a witness, but rather that all prophecy should be the same witness that Jesus gave.

This means that our prophetic listening should listen to God as Jesus listened to him, and that our prophetic words and deeds should point people to God as Jesus pointed them to God.

New Testament prophecy always focuses on what God is doing, thinking and saying – and not on a human response. Put simply, the early church's essential prophetic message to the Jews was, 'God is angry with you because you have rejected and crucified the *Messiah.*' The prophetic words pointed to God and his anger, not to the Jews.

As in the Old Testament, the early church's prophesying often encouraged a healthy fear of God: at times, the believers announced 'bad' news.

Only when the human response to their prophesying was, 'Then what can I do to be saved?' could evangelism effectively take place. It is this, not the prophecy, which points to the human response.

Prophecy and scripture

Some church leaders are opposed to personal and congregational prophecy, and they base their opposition on the supremacy of the Bible: they consider that prophecy must be either tautological or false.

Yet the book they seek to defend contains many encouragements to prophesy and many commendations of prophecy.

As we have seen, God's Written Word has a unique authority which can never be equalled. It is for all people, at all times, in all places – whereas prophecy is for a special person or group, in a particular place, at a specific time.

The biblical principle is plain: no prophecy must add to, or differ from, scripture: instead, every true prophecy is an essential, immediate supplement and application to scripture.

2 Peter 1:19 is unequivocal; yet its 'until' – and the reference in 1 Corinthians 13:8–9 to the end of imperfection – has led some to conclude that prophecy ceased with the completion of the Bible.

2 Peter 1:19 ☐

1 Corinthians 13:8–9 ☐

If this were true, however, we would also have to conclude that we lived in an age when all knowledge had ceased, the Day of the Lord had dawned, the Morning Star had come, and we could see Christ face-to-face!

Prophecy and opposition

The New Testament reminds us that the Old Testament prophets were rejected and persecuted, and promises this as the lot of all who prophesy. Matthew 5:11–12 and Luke 11:49 show this in part, but it is more fully developed in the book of Revelation.

Revelation 6:9 states that a very large number of saints will be killed because of the Word and their prophetic testimony to the Word. And Revelation 12:17 reveals the extreme opposition of the 'dragon' to those who obey God and bear witness – which includes prophetic listening and living – for Jesus.

PROPHETS IN THE EARLY CHURCH

Ephesians 4:7–16 shows that prophets were one of Christ's special gifts to the church after his ascension. He gave them to help build his church, and we consider them in *Glory in the Church*.

The prophets were not elected by the early church, nor chosen by the elders; they were those men or women whom the church leaders recognised as regularly receiving and delivering prophecies from God. They were simply those who prophesied more frequently than the rest.

The prophets normally occupy the second place after the apostles, and Ephesians 2:20 teaches that this is because of their part in the church's foundation. Ephesians 3:5 reveals that, along with apostles, prophets reveal the mystery, unknown to previous generations, which pagans share in the inheritance of Israel. This suggests that prophets have an important role to play in the establishment of new churches.

In Acts 13:1–3, the Antioch prophets were at worship when they were charged by the Holy Spirit with consecrating Barnabas and Saul to the task that he had already revealed to them. Their inward call was now confirmed by the prophets' outward call.

Just as the Old Testament prophets anointed the kings and set them apart for ruling, so the early church prophets laid hands on the ministers and consecrated them for serving. 1 Timothy 1:18; 4:14 and 2 Timothy 1:6 illustrate this.

Matthew 5:11–12 ☐
Luke 11:49 ☐

Revelation 6:9 ☐
12:17 ☐

Ephesians 4:7–16 ☐

Ephesians 2:20 ☐
3:5 ☐

Acts 13:1–3 ☐

1 Timothy 1:18 ☐
4:14 ☐
2 Timothy 1:6 ☐

In Acts 21:10–14, the prophet Agabus visited Paul, and – with both a prophetic action and prophetic words – warned Paul of what was to take place. The prophecy was not to prevent Paul from going to Jerusalem, but to warn him of what would happen. This divine insight meant that Paul was spiritually and mentally prepared when the riot began, and that he recognised the will of God in his circumstances.

Agabus also echoed the cries for social justice of his prophetic forebears, in Acts 11:27–30, when he revealed the Spirit's great interest in famine relief. Stirred by the Spirit, Agabus predicted the great famine of AD 49–50 which swept westwards through the Roman empire. This insight enabled the church to make adequate preparation.

Again, we must note that Agabus pointed essentially to what God was doing. He did not demand a human response to his prophecy; he did not instruct the people to take up a collection – he simply warned them to prepare for a coming famine. This, with its echo of Genesis 41, is real famine relief – it provides *before* the shortage occurs.

These verses demonstrate that the prophets in the early church were:

- *official* – their office was recognised by church leaders

- *translocal* – they travelled from church to church

- *inspired* – they were anointed and inspired by the Holy Spirit

- *predictive* – they announced what God was going to do

- *directive* – they directed the believers to act in specific ways

- *practical* – they were concerned with very practical matters

- *revelatory* – they taught God's Word

THE GIFT OF PROPHECY

The New Testament introduces the gift of prophecy to the church. This is a special gift of the Holy Spirit, and is just one aspect of prophecy. It is not the sum total of prophecy, but it is a significant part.

As we will see, it is right to emphasise this gift – but not to the exclusion of the other aspects of prophecy.

Acts 21:10–14 ☐

Acts 11:27–30 ☐

We learn about this gift in 1 Corinthians 12 & 14. These chapters are set in the context of teaching about public worship, especially the Lord's Supper; this suggests that the gift of prophecy is the aspect of prophecy which is particularly relevant to the church's public meetings.

The key Greek verb of 1 Corinthians 14 is *oikodomeo*. This is usually translated as 'to edify', but it literally means 'to build together in order to build up'. If we long for the church to be built together and built up, we should pay special attention to this chapter.

Be zealous for prophecy

1 Corinthians 14:1, 12 & 39 instruct Christians believers actively to *zeloo* for prophecy. This is a strong Greek verb which means 'to have great zeal', or 'to crave'.

If we long for God to speak, we will make listening to him a higher priority. We do not demonstrate our 'craving' for prophecy by asking God to speak; we evidence it by listening to him more zealously – because we know that it is will and nature to reveal his Word to us.

Prophecy addresses people

1 Corinthians 14:3 shows that the essential direction of the gift of prophecy is from God to people.

When the words of our God-ward prayers and worship are truly inspired by the Spirit, it is not wrong to describe them as 'prophetic'. This passage, however, deals with that aspect of prophecy – the spiritual gift – which is entirely human-ward in direction.

In the past, some churches failed to distinguish between *diermeneuo*, 'to interpret', and *propheteuo* 'to prophesy'. 1 Corinthians 14:5 shows that tongues + interpretation is of equal value to prophecy, but that it is not the equivalent of prophecy. Both gifts build the church, but verses 2–3 show that they do this from opposite directions.

Whenever we pray in tongues, or interpret a tongue, or manifest any spiritual gift, there is some element of prophetic speaking – for we have listened to God and are speaking his words in gospel obedience. But we are not exercising the particular 'gift' of prophecy – for this is the exclusively human-ward element within the broad topic of prophecy.

Prophecy builds, exhorts and comforts:

1 Corinthians 14:3 shows that the gift of prophecy brings:

- *oikodome* – edification: the gift is positive, not negative; it builds us together to build us up in the church

- *paraklesis* – exhortation: it reveals what God is doing and calls us to fall in step with this, to come alongside God in what he is doing

- *paramuthia* – comfort: it is 'near speech'; it is God whispering a tender message of comfort to friends and servants

Prophecy builds others

Prophecy is a self-giving, self-emptying gift. 1 Corinthians 14:4 states that those who prophesy do not aim to build themselves up; instead, they build together and build up the members of the church.

(Of course, as part of the church, they are themselves built up by their prophesying – but this is not their intention.)

Prophecy is a positive, constructive gift; it does not destroy or knock down. This is emphasised in verse 26.

Prophecy is important

1 Corinthians 14:5 shows that prophecy is important, and that we must not treat it casually. We are called to respect those men and women to whom God has entrusted a particular message for that occasion.

Prophecy is not necessarily spontaneous

1 Corinthians 14:26 suggests that the members of the church should spend time carefully preparing themselves for the services, listening to God for any contribution he wishes them to bring to the worship.

This means that any spiritual contribution – a song, talk, tongue, interpretation, prophecy, and so on – can be given by the Spirit in advance.

1 Corinthians 14:30 shows, however, that there is a real place for spontaneous prophecy in public worship.

Prophecy is revelatory

1 Corinthians 14:26 lists *apokalupsis* among the contributions that believers can bring to a service. This is usually translated as 'revelation' and means the unveiling, the revealing, of something which had previously been unknown: it clearly refers to prophecies.

Thus far, we have referred to prophecy as the 'now' Word of God. *Apokalupsis* means that we can, perhaps, also describe prophecy as the 'new' Word of God.

Of course, no prophecy is ever new to God; it is always utterly consistent with the nature and Word of God as expressed in Scripture and in line with the witness of Jesus. At times, however, a prophetic revelation will be new to us – in the sense that it is a fresh unveiling of one aspect of the eternal, unchanging Word.

Prophecy must be judged

1 Corinthians 14:29–32 makes it clear that prophecy must be judged or tested. We consider this in Part Eight.

Prophecy is for every believer

1 Corinthians 14:31 stresses that this gift is for *all* believers. Since Pentecost, all who have been anointed with the Spirit – who keep on listening to God and responding with gospel obedience – can prophecy. This will happen when churches start to be zealous for prophecy – and when they evidence this by making prophetic listening a higher priority.

Decently and in order

1 Corinthians 14:40 teaches that 'all things' – including the gift of prophecy – must be done with:

- *euschemonos* – this means we should prophecy with beauty, or gracefully, and not in an uncontrolled or unhelpful manner.

- *taxis* – this means our services should have an order, a deliberate arrangement, with a proper, appropriate and recognised place for 'all things' – including prophecy. This *taxis* can be arranged by the leader with the help of the gift of wisdom.

OTHER REVELATION GIFTS

1 Corinthians 12–14 refers to three other gifts which God gives to provide us with prophetic revelation, or 'spiritual eyesight'.

The word of knowledge

Through this gift, the Spirit reveals facts to us about a person or situation. This is not insight which comes through the natural mind, reason, experience or instinct; instead, it is a freely-given fragment of God's own knowledge.

By this gift, God discloses a truth which the Spirit wishes to be made known.

We see this, for example, in 2 Kings 5:20–27; 6:9–12; 2 Samuel 12:1–7; Matthew 9:1–7; 17:27; John 4:7–25; 4:45–54; Acts 5:1–6 and 9:11.

The word of wisdom

This gift is the Spirit-given insight as to how a revelation should be best applied in a specific situation, or how a particular person or situation is best helped.

We can say that the word of wisdom is the Spirit's 'how' and the word of knowledge is his 'what'.

We see examples of this gift in: Genesis 41:14–45; 1 Kings 3:16–28; 2 Kings 5:8–14; Matthew 21:23–27; 22:15–22; Luke 21:15; John 8:7.

The discerning of spirits

This is the God-given perception which enables a believer to identify the motivating spirit behind particular words or deeds: it helps us to grasp the involvement of the human spirit, a demonic spirit and the Holy Spirit.

We see this, for example, in 1 Samuel 3:1–9; 16:6–13; Matthew 16:21–23; Luke 13:10–17; Acts 5:1–11; 8:14–24; 13:4–12; 16:16–18.

We consider the special part that this gift plays in the judging of prophecy in Part Eight.

Let prophetic gifts happen

Prophetic revelation and insight, including the gift of prophecy, built the early church – and it still builds the church today.

If 'church-building' is our heart's desire, we will follow 1 Corinthians 14:40 and allow the revelation gifts to *ginomai*. This is usually translated as 'be done', but 'become', or 'come into being', or 'happen' is more accurate.

We do not worship a dumb God. There is no gag in his mouth. We do not need to implore him to speak. Instead, we must extract the spiritual cotton wool from our ears which blocks out his voice and start listening to him with greater care and intensity.

PART SEVEN

prophetic listening today

We have seen that prophecy involves a complete process from God's gracious initiation of his Word to our obedient application of the Word. Like conversion, faith and listening, prophecy involves several stages – it is not one quick event. For example, prophecy involves:

- *listening* – we must listen actively to God to hear what he is saying

- *revelation* – God reveals his particular message in one of the many different ways that he uses to communicate his Word and will

- *interpretation* – the revelation can come in a variety of forms, so great care is needed to ensure that the Word is understood correctly

- *application* – we must listen actively to God to learn from him how to handle his *rhema* Word, whom to give it to, when to pass it on, and so on

- *motivation* – we must remind ourselves that the primary purpose of all revelation is to know God better, and ensure that we do not have any ungodly, critical or self-seeking reasons for prophesying

- *testing* – every Word must be offered for testing, judging, weighing, sifting; nobody should ever insist that a word must be received and obeyed without any form of testing

- *communication* – the Word must be delivered in God's way, and with his grace, order and gentle authority

- *action* – the Word must be obeyed and acted upon, so that it can achieve God's creative purpose and produce its appointed fruit

Passages like 1 Corinthians 2:9–16 and Isaiah 55:6–11 illustrate the inherent divine power of the full prophetic process: we surely need to seek God for a restoration of this *authentic* prophetic ministry to the church today.

A trinitarian base

When we consider prophetic listening, we need to keep on reminding ourselves that it has a thoroughly trinitarian foundation.

- *The Father initiates every Word. He is the communicating God who speaks to make himself known and to bring life and salvation to the whole world.*

- *The Son is himself the Personal Word: he is the full, eternal revelation of God's holy name and nature.*

- *The Holy Spirit is the Spirit of revelation. He has inspired the Written Word so that it is the full, complete, sufficient and infallible record of what God has communicated. He witnesses directly to our spirits, testifies to Jesus, and speaks to us through the prophetic word.*

We see this trinitarian activity in Psalm 115:2–7; John 1:1–3; 14:10; 15:26; 16:13–15; 17:1–3; Romans 5:5; 8:9, 15–16; 1 Corinthians 12:7, 10; 14:3–4; Galatians 4:6; 2 Timothy 3:16–17 and Revelation 19:10.

A scriptural foundation

We also need to remember that the Spirit communicates through the Written Word of God, through the Bible. 2 Timothy 3:17 makes it plain that God is still breathing the Scriptures to us today, still speaking them into our personal and congregational lives.

Sidebar references: 1 Corinthians 2:9–16; Isaiah 55:6–11; Psalm 115:2–7; John 1:1–3; 14:10; 15:26; 16:13–15; 17:1–3; Romans 5:5; 8:9; 8:15–16; 1 Corinthians 12:7, 10; 14:3–4; Galatians 4:6; 2 Timothy 3:16–17; Revelation 19:10

We can say that the Spirit:

- *illuminates* – he brings understanding of the Scriptures

- *confirms* – he bears witness to the Scriptures through inner witness, personal assurance and signs and wonders

- *illustrates* – he draws attention to biblical principles, and shows which Scriptures are significant to particular situations

- *applies* – he applies the Scriptures to believers' lives by bringing out the specific prophetic relevance of a verse or passage to those who will hear and accept it

Prophecy is one of the ways that the Spirit illuminates, confirms, illustrates and applies the Scriptures. We can say that he uses congregational prophecy to speak to a particular church or group, and personal prophecy to speak to an individual.

A balanced view

Some people seem to suggest that personal and congregational prophecy are *everything* – every word is received directly and infallibly from God, and should be accepted without question. While others insist that prophecy, especially personal prophecy, is *nothing* – every word is only a human opinion and should be valued accordingly.

The biblical position, however, seems to be that personal and congregational prophecy are *something*: when they are properly weighed and tested, they are part of God's Word to us – and should be obeyed and acted upon as such.

No prophecy should be accepted hastily or uncritically, nor should it be acted upon unwisely: rather, it must be regulated, tested and acted upon with sanctified common sense and wisdom. It is only *one way* that God speaks to us today, but it is *a way* that he does speak.

1 Thessalonians 5:19–21 neatly summarises the biblical attitude:

1 Thessalonians 5:19–21 ☐

- *do not quench the Spirit*

- *do not despise prophecies*

- *test everything*

- *hold fast to that which is good*

When we draw together the biblical principles we have considered so far, we can see that there are three main aspects of prophecy which should be found within the church today.

1.   *the prophetic role* – every believer is called to listen and live prophetically, both individually and together in the church. This is the 'prophet-hood of all believers' which, since Pentecost, belongs to everyone who has been anointed with the Spirit.

Acts 2:17–18 ☐

Hebrews 8:10–11 ☐

1 John 2:27 ☐

We see this in Acts 2:17–18; Hebrews 8:10–11 & 1 John 2:27.

2.   *the prophetic gift* – every believer may, from time to time, be inspired by the Spirit to give a prophetic message. This manifestation of the gift of prophecy takes the form of a specific word of edification, exhortation or comfort, and either operates *congregationally* – within public worship – or *personally* – in private ministry, personal conversation, or public worship.

John 4:16–19, 29 ☐

1 Corinthians
12:10 ☐
14:1–5 ☐
14:24–25 ☐
14:29–32 ☐

Acts 13:2, 9–12 ☐

We see these two aspects of the gift in John 4: 16–19, 29; 1 Corinthians 12:10; 14:1–5, 24–25, 29–32; Acts 13:2, 9–12.

3.   *the prophetic ministry* – there are particular men and women who are recognised as prophets. The prophetic gift is particularly developed in, and frequently manifested through, these people.

Ephesians 4:11 ☐

Acts 11:27–28 ☐
13:1 ☐
15:32 ☐

We see this in Ephesians 4:11; Acts 11:27–28; 13:1 & 15:32.

THE PROPHETIC ROLE

We have seen that every believer has a prophetic function to fulfil, and this effects every area of their lives. An intimate prophetic relationship with God, which involves prophetic listening, is the only reliable foundation for all our speaking and serving.

Every book in this *Sword of the Spirit* series is implicitly founded on the principle of prophetic listening to God. For example:

Romans 8:26–27 ☐

1 Corinthians
14:24–25 ☐

Ephesians
5:17–20 ☐

1 Peter 2:9 ☐

In *Worship in Spirit and Truth*, we establish that all our prayer, praise, worship and service has a prophetic dimension – even though it is God-ward in direction. We see this in Romans 8:26–27; 1 Corinthians 14:24–25; Ephesians 5:17–20 & 1 Peter 2:9.

In *Reaching the Lost*, we note that the gospel is to be declared in prophetic power, inspiration and miraculous confirmation. We see this, for example, in John 1:47–50; 4:5–26; Romans 15:17–21; 1 Corinthians 2:1–5; Ephesians 6:19–20; 1 Thessalonians 1:4–10 & Hebrews 2:1–4.

And in *Living Faith* and *Ministry in the Spirit*, we note how prophetic words of faith are spoken to people and situations which need to be changed so that God's kingdom purposes can be fulfilled. We see this, for example in Matthew 17:14–20; Mark 9:23 & 11:22–25.

In one sense, the very existence of the Christian community is a prophetic sign of the kingdom of God. Just as the lives of the Old Testament prophets communicated something of God to the people around them, so the corporate life of the church today is a revelation of God's character and purposes.

We note, in *The Rule of God*, that Jesus' 'Sermon on the Mount' is the manifesto of his kingdom. In this sermon, in Matthew 5:13–16, Jesus uses 'salt' and 'light' as prophetic pictures to reveal the marks of the church, his kingdom people. And, in Luke 10:3, he charges his disciples with serving as 'lambs among wolves'. These three pictures illustrate the whole church's vital prophetic role today.

Salt

The phrase 'the salt of the world' suggests that the entire church has a prophetic function in social purification. Today, we use salt mainly for flavouring, but in Jesus' day it was used both to preserve from decay and to purify that which had decayed. We see this in, for example, Leviticus 2:13; 2 Kings 2:20 and Ezekiel 16:4.

The church has this twin prophetic role of preserving our society from further decay and of purifying that which has already become decadent. This shows that we must be deeply involved in society, and that our listening must not focus only on church affairs.

Light

The expression 'the light of the world' suggests that the church should be a means of prophetic illumination and revelation in the world. Together, we should live in obedience to the Word of God and bring

John 1:47–50 ☐
4:5–26 ☐

Romans
15:17–21 ☐

1 Corinthians
2:1–5 ☐

Ephesians
6:19–20 ☐

1 Thessalonians
1:4–10 ☐

Hebrews 2:1–4 ☐

Matthew
17:14–20 ☐

Mark 9:23 ☐
11:22–25 ☐

Matthew
5:13–16 ☐

Luke 10:3 ☐

Leviticus 2:13 ☐

2 Kings 2:20 ☐

Ezekiel 16:4 ☐

the light of the Word to shine on society – and so reveal the true nature of its problems.

We know that the Old Testament prophets spoke when the Word of the Lord came to them. Our corporate listening to the Word, and our gospel acceptance and obedience to the Word, should lead to a prophetic revelation of the Word to the world.

Lambs

Jesus' picture of 'lambs among wolves' indicates the need for God's prophetic people to live out their 'servant' nature. We know that 'the' prophet mighty in word and deed was himself the Lamb of God, and that his flock enters and lives in his kingdom by the same 'lamb' principle of self-sacrifice and service.

Most people in the world want to be 'wolves'; few want to lie down and be 'lambs'. It is essential, however, that Christ's followers take care not to dominate others. We are called to accept the domination of others and daily to offer our lives as a sacrifice pleasing to God – united with the sacrifice of Jesus.

Following on from the biblical principles of prophecy, we can say that the whole church has a prophetic role to play in these areas.

Reconciliation

The church will be prophetic only when reconciliation is a visible feature of its life and message. Our reconciliation with God must be demonstrated by genuine reconciliation in the church, within-and-between local congregations, and by a continuing message of reconciliation to-and-in the world.

This reconciliation is important – in the family, between husbands and wives, and parents and children; at work, between employer and employee; in society, between black and white, rich and poor, north and south, employed and unemployed, landlord and tenant, and so on.

Unholy divisions in the body of Christ deny the message of reconciliation and must be called sin. Alienation and discord within the church need to be identified and healed so that the whole church can be a prophetic reconciled community.

As God's judgement is poured on society, the prophetic church needs to proclaim the timeless message, 'Get right with God and get right with each other.' We need to consider ourselves as a prophetic 'counter-culture' which listens for God's Word on these issues.

Justice and compassion

We have seen that the Old Testament prophets demonstrated and prophesied for God's justice and compassion in their society. They told people that God wanted the poor to be cared for; and they announced God's curse upon those who were apathetic to the poor, and his blessing upon those who made generous provision.

This concern was echoed by the early church – and it should be seen and heard today throughout the church. As the Christian community, we have a particular responsibility for the poor and oppressed, and are called to identify with the needy within our nation and world.

A prophetic church should articulate God's thoughts, not its own ideas, about justice and social issues. This means that we need to take great care that we listen to his Word rather than to our own culture.

National events

We have seen that the prophets of old were often summoned by their rulers to reveal God's thoughts about the events and issues of the day. So too, the prophetic people of God today need to pass on God's thoughts about contemporary issues.

Together, we should be prayerfully listening for God's thoughts about social, local, national and international issues. As churches, we must prophetically hear and speak God's present 'burdens' for our communities. When churches have done this in the past, revival has often followed. It is the New Testament principle that prophecy prepares the way for the effective proclamation of the good news.

The real enemy

Monotheism was the relentless cry of biblical prophets. Today, this involves pointing out the real enemy, so that the church and the nation are not side-tracked by religious, economic or sociological distractions.

The Bible reveals that we have two genuine enemies: Satan and death. As God's prophetic people, our role is to point people away from these enemies. The evil one, however seeks to distract us from this task by continually suggesting false enemies.

At various times, some sections of the church have been led astray and have attacked Turks, Jews, Anabaptists, Lollards, Catholics, Protestants, Methodists, Negroes, Americans, Communists, and so on.

A prophetic church, however, needs to listen carefully to God to learn how Satan is working today and to discern how his intrigues should be exposed and opposed. The real enemy behind the supposed enemy must be recognised in order to avoid false, human remedies – which are always spiritually counter-productive. This can be recognised only through prophetic listening.

Servants

The church will fulfil its prophetic role only when servanthood becomes central to its way of life. We know that all biblical prophets were servants; even Jesus came to serve and demonstrated this by washing his disciples' feet.

Matthew
  20:20–28 ☐
  23:2–23 ☐

If the church is to be prophetic, the words of Matthew 20:20–28 and 23:2–23 must be applied, and the love of power, position and status must be cast out from our midst.

Jesus' words in Matthew 23:8–12 are a great indictment of our age. The world may be changed by politics and political weapons, but these are not God's way for a serving church.

Our prophetic weapons are truth, not advertising; righteousness and justice, not violence; peace-filled submission, not a power struggle; faith, not ideology; salvation, not idealism; the Word of God, not good public relations; intercession, not well-meaning actions.

Intercession

The Old Testament prophets were the intercessors of their day. If the church is to be prophetic, effective, persistent intercession must come centre stage again. If we care enough to prophesy, we must care enough to pray. We consider this in *Effective Prayer*.

THE PROPHETIC GIFT

We have noted that the prophetic role is for all believers, all the time, whereas the gift of prophecy is a particular manifestation of the Spirit which is given to a specific person for a particular purpose. We can say that the prophetic role is the normal Christian life, but that the prophetic gift is part of the Christian life.

The gift of prophecy is one of the 'grace-gifts' of the Spirit. As we have established throughout this series, all the different gifts are genuine freely-given gifts, not rewards or trophies; they are all tools for use, not toys for entertainment; and they are all initiated by the Spirit, not abilities to perform at will.

1 Corinthians 14:3 establishes that the gift of prophecy is given by the Spirit so that God can build, exhort and comfort people. Like all the other gifts, this evidences the real partnership which exists between God and anointed believers.

1 Corinthians
14:3 ☐

The manifestation of the gift

Every manifestation of the gift is initiated by the Holy Spirit, yet it is also subject to the person's will. We cannot prophecy simply at will, yet God does not over-ride our will and make us prophecy.

We have seen that the New Testament teaches that this is a gift which God gives to anointed believers. This means that we can expect him to give this gift whenever we gather together *congregationally* to build, exhort and comfort each other, and whenever we need it *personally* in Spirit-directed ministry.

• *congregational prophecy*

1 Corinthians 14 suggests that we should come together with a quiet confidence that God will manifest the gift of prophecy among us – and we can all expect him sometimes to manifest it personally through us. God's desire is to build and bless others through us, so we should always be listening to the Spirit in case he wants to use us today.

Of course, our prophetic listening should not start with the opening song of a service. We need to listen to God throughout the week – at home and at work, at rest and at play – because God speaks when he chooses to speak, and not just when we ask him to speak.

1 Corinthians 14:26 suggests that we should come to public worship both prepared to contribute *and* with a prepared contribution.

The Spirit may speak to us during a meeting and prompt us to prophesy: he may even provide us with the words as we prophesy. At other times, however, he provides us with the essence of the prophetic message days in advance, and we have then to speak this at the appointed point in the meeting.

When two or three believers prophesy spontaneously, and their messages are similar, it is inevitable that some people will wonder how much the second and third prophecies were influenced by the content of the first.

God does speak in this way, but he knows that it is somehow more compelling – especially for unbelievers – when several people bring similar prepared prophetic messages which they received independently in the previous week.

• *personal prophecy*

We have seen that, in the New Testament, some manifestations of the gift of prophecy are *personal* rather than *corporate*, as in Acts 21:11; that others are *private* rather than *public*, as in John 4:16–19; and that a few can be *personal* yet *public*, as in 1 Corinthians 14:24–25.

God speaks in this direct and personal way to show a person that Jesus knows them individually and cares about them personally – we can say that, within every genuine personal prophecy, there is a call to embrace and follow Christ.

Passages like Romans 1:11–12; 1 Timothy 1:18; 4:13–14; 2 Timothy 1:6–7 make it plain that personal prophecy can activate the gifts and ministries of the Holy Spirit in a particular believer's life.

This involves both *revelation* – supernatural knowledge about the person's situation and need, or about the ministry and gift that the Spirit is imparting, and also *release* – supernatural enabling and equipping with faith, boldness, power, courage and determination to fulfil the prophetic word.

Personal prophecy, like all manifestations of the gift of prophecy, is given expressly to build up by building together the body of Christ. Instead of demolishing and condemning people, it builds them up and encourages them. We see this in 1 Corinthians 14:3.

1 Corinthians
14:3 ☐

And we have seen that personal prophecy brings specific direction and helpful information to people for their lives and ministries – for example, Acts 11:27–30; 21:4, 10–14.

Acts 11:27–30 ☐
21:4 ☐
21:10–14 ☐

Of course, there will always be some people who misuse the gift of prophecy in an attempt to control and manipulate others; but this should not stop us from seeking to use it correctly. The devil is firmly opposed to prophecy, and he is equally pleased with those believers who reject it and those who misuse it.

We must be those who are open to personal and congregational prophecy, but who deal with it in a thoroughly biblical manner.

Order in the exercise of the gift

The whole Bible encourages prophecy, and the thrust of 1 Corinthians 12–14 is that spiritual gifts in general, and prophecy in particular, should be eagerly and zealously sought – provided that this is done in the right way and for the right reasons.

Quite simply, every single believer should be very keen to prophesy – because this gift encourages, instructs, challenges, comforts and builds the body of Christ.

1 Corinthians 14:26 shows that a love-inspired longing for the blessing, benefit and building of others is the only acceptable motive for the exercise of any spiritual gift. All forms of ostentatious spirituality, pride, ambition, attention-seeking and self-glorification are totally repugnant to the humble, self-effacing Holy Spirit.

1 Corinthians
14:26 ☐

We may listen to God carefully, hear him clearly, even speak his words accurately, but the prophecy will not be honoured by God if we deliver it proudly – hoping to attract attention to ourselves and to make some sort of name for ourselves as a spiritual person.

It is vital we appreciate that the principle of human partnership with God means that no manifestation of a gift is infallible. The New Testament is clear: every prophetic manifestation must be judged. Clearly this would not be necessary if manifestations were infallible;

and we consider this in Part Eight. This means that one mark of prophetic genuineness is an obvious willingness by the believer manifesting the gift to submit their words to scrutiny. Prophecies should not be expressed in words, and in a style, which seem to claim infallibility and question the need for testing.

Some leaders have suggested that, today, no prophecy should ever be brought in the first person; but this is not the real issue. It is usually a matter of culture and background whether a person expresses a prophecy in terms of, 'Thus says the Lord...', or, 'I think that God might be saying something like this...'. We must remember that Ezekiel's prophecies were much more forthright than Nathan's, and accept that one style of prophesying may be relevant to one culture and quite unacceptable in another.

The real issue is whether a person claims infallibility for their words and rejects the need for testing. This can be asserted in very subtle ways, and some 'third person' prophecies can be far more 'controlling' than most 'first person' prophecies.

1 Corinthians
14:32–33 ☐

1 Corinthians 14:32–33 shows that the gift of prophecy should not be exercised in some uncontrolled ecstasy or frenzy. Self-control is as much an evidence of the Spirit's presence as any spiritual gift.

In some traditions, people seem to become over-intense in their pursuit of this gift, and to manifest the gift in a way which suggests that they have no control over they way they prophesy. This is not God's way, and it leads to spurious manifestations and a striving which negates the essential nature of prophecy as a 'grace-gift'.

We cannot 'work up' any gift; instead, they well up through the operation of the Holy Spirit within us. We must simply learn to be attentive to the Spirit, and to be ready to be used by him – as, how and when he wills. Anything else is manufactured and fake.

The prophetic spirit is our new birthright, and we move out in the gift of prophecy when we:

- *wait on the Lord*

- *look to him in quiet expectation*

- *listen attentively to him*

- *speak out what we hear with humility*

- *submit our words for judging*

THE PROPHETIC MINISTRY

In *Glory in the Church*, we consider the Ephesians 4:11–13 gifts which the ascended Christ has given for the building of his church, and note that this passage shows these ministries are needed until the work of church building is completed. This means that all these ministries – including the prophet – should be recognised and accepted today.

Ephesians
4:11–13 ☐

All the Ephesians 4:11 ministries are based on listening to God for his Word and will – as these disciplines are fundamental to all Christian service. But, if it is possible, the prophetic ministry is somehow even more dependent on careful listening than the other ministries.

Ephesians 2:20 shows that 'foundation' apostles and prophets had a unique calling to reveal the gospel and to establish the early church. The church has been established, and their revelation is now recorded in the New Testament. Their initial foundation actions are full-and-final; there is no need for any contemporary prophetic ministry on the same 'ultimate establishing and revelatory' lines.

Ephesians 2:20 ☐

This does not mean, however, that there is no place for the prophetic ministry today. As we note in *Glory in the Church*, prophets make a special and unique contribution to the on-going building of the church, and to establishing new congregations and revealing God's Word.

God uses prophets today to confront us with the reality of his particular will, and to give us his direction, wisdom, instruction, warning, guidance and insight.

In fact, we can say that it is through his servants the prophets that God stirs the church into action. Whereas pastors and teachers aim for a settled ministry, the prophets stir and exhort us into service.

Revelation is the key element in all biblical prophetic ministry – a revelation which emphasises the immediate message of the Lord which the prophet has heard in his intimate personal relationship with God. There seem to be five aspects to this revelation.

Prophets bring revelation from Scripture

The Ephesians 4:11 ministries have distinctive, but complementary, purposes in communicating God's Word from the Bible.

- *apostles* – minister the Word which brings foundational structure to newly planted churches

- *evangelists* – speak the Word which brings people to faith in Christ

- *pastors* – encourage, comfort and nurture believers in the Word

- *teachers* – bring the Word which instructs and informs believers

- *prophets* – deliver the Word which challenges, exhorts, builds and comforts – with a distinctive revelatory content

Prophets do not just bring a general Word from God, they also unburden the particular Word from Scripture which is relevant for that unique group of people at that specific time. We can say that teachers deal with systematics, and prophets deal in specifics; that teachers bring a balanced 'diet', and prophets bring a particular 'diet' which deals with a specific 'nutritional' deficiency.

All believers need both the regular biblical teaching and systematic scriptural exposition of teachers *and* the focused revelation of prophets. All the Ephesians 4:11 ministries complement each other, and some of them can be found in the same person.

Prophets bring revelation for people

We have seen that personal revelation is an undoubted aspect of the prophetic ministry. There has been some controversy about this in recent years, but the potential pitfalls can be avoided when prophets minister with humility, in real relationship with other Ephesians 4:11 ministries, and in submission to the local elders wherever they minister.

This personal revelation takes many different forms, for example:

2 Samuel
12:1–10 ☐

- *2 Samuel 12:1–10* – a confrontation with a believer's sin: this must not be 'spiritual slander'; its aim is to build, not to tear down.

John 4:16–19 ☐

1 Corinthians
14:24–25 ☐

- *John 4:16–19; 1 Corinthians 14:24–25* – a revelation to a non-believer: this must be positive and evangelistic, not negative and judgmental.

Acts 21:4, 10–15 ☐

- *Acts 21:4, 10–15* – a prediction to a believer: we must distinguish between truly inspired warnings which mean to prepare us, and less-than-inspired advice which only seems to be prophetic.

- *1 Timothy 1:18–19; 4:14; 2 Timothy 1:6* – a spiritual gifting can take place through the laying on of hands and prophetic direction: we consider this in *Ministry in the Spirit.*

1 Timothy
1:18–19 ☐
4:14 ☐

2 Timothy 1:6 ☐

Prophets bring revelation for the church

We have seen that prophets are particularly charged with building the church, and they do this by bringing a specific revelation which gives direction about God's way forward in, for example, evangelism, ministry, intercession, and other aspects of church life.

Jesus is the head of the church, and he still makes his will known to his body through prophetic revelation and direction. We see this in Acts 13:1–3, where the prophetic message for Paul and Barnabas had considerable implications for the church at Antioch. It is important we recognise that the personal revelation here was given in the corporate context of the church and leaders.

Acts 13:1–3 ☐

The prophetic revelation in Revelation 1–3 is characterised by the phrase, 'Hear what the Spirit says to the churches'. This shows that God speaks through anointed prophets directly to particular churches.

Revelation 1–3 ☐

The voice of the Spirit in these three chapters is diagnostic and healing, encouraging and directional, chastening and comforting. In the same way, we need to listen to his voice today when he speaks through the prophets – and to receive the Word sensitively, and to implement it faithfully.

Prophets bring revelation on the future

We have seen that prophets in the Old Testament and the early church sometimes brought God's insight into the future – as, for example, in Isaiah 41:22–23; 48:5–7; Acts 11:27–30; 20:22–24. Revelation about the future is still part of the prophetic ministry, but we should avoid idle curiosity and sensationalism.

Isaiah 41:22–23 ☐
48:5–7 ☐

Acts 11:27–30 ☐
20:22–24 ☐

Deuteronomy 18:21–22 reveals that the acid test of a predictive prophecy is whether or not it is fulfilled. Some people make sweeping predictions which cannot be tested in this way – especially about great blessing or the events at the end of our age. If their 'guess' has not yet been fulfilled, they insist that it will be later on.

Deuteronomy
18:21–22 ☐

But, strictly speaking, biblical predictive prophecy is always specific and never vague: it is either obviously fulfilled or it is clearly false. We need to recognise that, today, many prophetic manifestations are 'immature' or 'incomplete' rather than 'false'.

The people bringing them have heard something genuine from God, but they have not persisted in their prophetic listening to hear from him more completely.

Many of us seem to be too easily satisfied with superficial prophesying and incomplete ministering, when God wants us to persist in listening to him so that he can draw us deeper into himself. Only then will we hear his quietest whispers.

Prophets bring revelation to the nation

Although it is clear that the Old Testament prophets declared God's Word to the nations, the prophets in the early church do not appear to have ministered in the same way. This has led some leaders to argue that this aspect of the prophetic ministry ceased with Christ.

All church leaders agree that the church should prophetically address society through evangelism, witness, service and protest; but many leaders are not sure about the precise nature of the prophetic ministry to the nations. The Bible does not provide us with clear guidance on this matter.

When we consider this issue, we need to remember these points.

- The Old Testament prophets declared God's Word essentially to a theocratic state – to God's covenant people living as a nation. Therefore, we might not be able to use their example as a model in this aspect of prophecy.

- At times, however, the prophets did speak to other nations and reveal God's attitude to unbelieving societies – including secular states and those controlled by false religions. We see this in Isaiah 13–23; Jeremiah 1:5; 46–51; Amos 1:3–2:3; Jonah 1–4.

- God does deal with nations – we see this in *Knowing the Father* – and there is no indication that this is no longer true today. For example, Romans 11 makes it plain that God still has considerable purposes for Israel.

Isaiah 13–23 ☐

Jeremiah 1:5 ☐

1:46–51 ☐

Amos 1:3–2:3 ☐

Jonah 1–4 ☐

Romans 11 ☐

It does not seem right to deny the supernatural element in the prophetic Word to our desperately needy nations. God can and does still give prophetic revelation which is of national and international significance. As the church grows in maturity, this may become an increasing part of the prophetic ministry.

We surely need prophetic ministers who will speak God's general Word to the nations about social, political and spiritual issues, and will declare his particular Word about specific national and international events.

PART EIGHT

judging revelation

Throughout the Old Testament era, God spoke to people through his listening servants, the anointed prophets. They progressively brought God's personal revelation to Israel, and their words – being the very Word of God – were infallible.

Despite this, the prophets' revelation of God was always limited and incomplete. The full-and-final revelation of God to humanity could be brought only through-and-by the Personal Word of God – the supreme prophet, the beloved divine Son, the suffering servant of God.

By the end of the New Testament era, God had communicated his Word fully and completely to humanity. This revelation was recorded in the Written Word of God – which is God's sufficient, authoritative, out-breathed, infallible record for all people at all times.

Because of this, we do not judge – indeed we dare not judge – the Written Word of God; instead, we accept it, we submit to it, we obey it, and we ourselves are judged by it.

We see this in Hebrews 1:1–2; 2 Timothy 3:15–17; 2 Peter 1:3–4, 19–21; and we consider it more fully in *Living Faith*.

Hebrews 1:1–2 ☐

2 Timothy
3:15–17 ☐

2 Peter 1:3–4 ☐
1:19–21 ☐

This means that, since the time of the early church in the book of Acts, no prophetic revelation has carried – or can carry – the same level of inspiration and infallibility as Scripture.

LEVELS OF INSPIRATION

We may be convinced that we have heard God speaking to us personally, clearly, and in a quite wonderful way; we may be sure that we know God's will and particular *rhema* Word for our situation. But we must also be absolutely certain that the revelation which we have heard or received can not be as inspired and infallible as the Bible, and that it – therefore – must always be judged in a way that Scripture must never be judged.

In the times of the early church, apostolic prophecy was given for the purpose of laying down doctrinal guidance for the whole church in all ages. This was authoritative revelation which was part of God's full-and-final Word to humanity.

It should be plain that no such revelation is given today: we must reject any revelation which purports to be fully inspired and infallible, and any which the messenger suggests should be accepted without any form of judging.

Since the apostolic era, God has continued to give prophetic revelation to build the church and further its work on earth. The level of inspiration, though, is much less, and the words which are given are for specific situations only, and are not binding – or even necessarily relevant – to the whole church.

We can see this lesser degree of inspiration in the New Testament.

- *In 1 Corinthians 14, for example, the gift of prophecy did not carry with it an inspiration which extended to the exact words spoken by the person prophesying. Instead, it seems that the Holy Spirit gave the essence of a revelation which was then expressed fallibly through the personality of the people prophesying.*

- *The 1 Corinthians 14 prophecies could contain error, and had to be submitted for scrutiny and judging.*

- *As there is no suggestion that the Corinthians prophecies were to be either recorded for posterity or passed on to other congregations, they were clearly not of universal importance. They were simply messages for those people at that time – and quite unlike Scripture or 'foundational' prophecies.*

- *1 Corinthians 14:30 implies that some prophesies should not be given, and that others should be given only in part. This proves that these 'gift' prophecies are less important than both Scripture and the 'foundational' prophetic utterances.*

1 Corinthians
14:30 ☐

- *Paul's words in 1 Corinthians 14:37–38 imply that Paul, as a personal apostle of Jesus, had an authority which was greater than that of those believers who prophesied in Corinth, and greater even than those who were recognised there as prophets.*

1 Corinthians
14:37–38 ☐

It is precisely because, today, we are involved in these lower levels of inspiration that we need to ensure that all the fruit of prophetic listening is judged according to biblical principles.

THE PURPOSE OF REVELATION

Whenever we consider a prophetic revelation, we need to remind ourselves about the three principle purposes of God's Word. If a revelation does not seem to share these purposes, we need to test it especially thoroughly.

1. To know God

We must never forget that the primary purpose of all revelation is to know God; anything else – direction, insight, prediction, empowering, comfort, edification, and so on – is secondary.

1 Samuel 3:7 ☐

God's revelation is always based in self-revelation – which is why the incarnate Personal Word is fundamental. God is the living God who 'speaks' and 'communicates' and reveals himself. His great longing is for all people, and each person, to know him and to be caught up in his purposes. We see this, for example, in 1 Samuel 3:7; Ephesians 1:17–18; Colossians 1:9–10 & 2:2–3.

Ephesians
1:17–18 ☐

Colossians
1:9–10 ☐
2:2–3 ☐

2.   To build the church

We must always remember that the church is built – or edified – by prophetic revelation, and that prophetic revelation is given to build the church together so that it can be built up.

Ephesians 2:20 ☐

We have seen, in Ephesians 2:20, that the church has been built on the foundation of the apostles and prophets. This is the once-and-for-all revelation which has been given by God.

There remains, however, a progressive building of the church – up into maturity, and out through evangelism – and God continues to provide revelation for this great building project.

1 Corinthians 14:3 ☐

And we have noted, in 1 Corinthians 14:3, that this 'church-building' revelation:

- *shows how God wants us to be built together and built up*

- *reveals what God is doing and calls us to fall in step with him – to come alongside God in what he is doing*

- *reminds us of God's love and comfort*

3.   To release power

We have seen that Jesus restricted himself to saying and doing only what he discerned the Father saying and doing through his prophetic listening. This means that there is a direct link between revelation and the release of God's power, between listening and loosing God's power in human lives.

As we see in *Living Faith* and *Ministry in the Spirit*, the works of the kingdom – evangelism, healing, deliverance, miracles and so on – are all carried out in the context of a revelation of God's particular Word concerning what the Father is doing, at that time and in that place.

Matthew 13:53–58 ☐

Luke 4:23–30 ☐

5:17 ☐

John 5:1–18 ☐

14:10 ☐

Acts 14:9–10 ☐

We know that we are called to share in Jesus' ministry, and that he is the model for all Christian ministry: this means that we must learn to speak and act only after receiving a divine revelation of the Father's words and actions in the course of our prophetic listening.

We see this, for example, in Matthew 13:53–58; Luke 4:23–30; 5:17; John 5:1–18; 14:10; Acts 14:9–10.

JUDGING REVELATION

We have constantly noted that we must test all the revelations which we hear – whether personally in our own listening to God or through the words of others who have listened to him. This is underlined by 1 Thessalonians 5:19–22, which commands us not to treat prophecies with contempt, to *test everything*, and to hold on to the good.

1 Thessalonians
5:19–22 ☐

It is almost impossible to overstate the importance of judging the fruit of prophetic listening: this is a vital means of avoiding error and receiving what God is really 'saying'. This judging involves a consideration and assessment of the content of the words, their motive and purpose, and the life of the speaker.

In the church today, there is a real fear of false prophets and false prophecy; superficial prophecy attracts less attention but it is equally dangerous and even more widespread. We need to distinguish between:

- *infallible prophecy* – This is the prophecy of Scripture and the foundation prophets which should not be judged.

- *false prophecy* – This is 'prophecy' whose motive, origin and content are totally foreign to the Spirit of Jesus; once recognised, this must be completely rejected.

- *impure prophecy* – This is prophecy where parts of the motive, origin and content are the product of the human servant. God has genuinely spoken; but his holy essence has been added to, or an ungodly motive has tainted its delivery, or it has been given at the wrong time, or in an uncontrolled manner.

  In this case, judging involves separating the human dross from the divine gold, and holding on only to that part which is good.

- *pure prophecy* – Within the limits of human fallibility, this is prophecy whose motive, origin and content are the product only of the Holy Spirit. Once tested and recognised, this must be fully accepted.

When we judge revelation, there are a series of tests which help us to establish whether a prophecy is false or pure, and there are some basic spiritual guidelines – and an important gift of the Spirit – which help us to 'separate' impure prophecy into its constituent parts.

Functional tests

Drawing on Ephesians 1:17; 1 Corinthians 14:5, 6, 12 & Deuteronomy 18:21–22, we can say that there are three simple questions which we need to ask about any revelation.

- *Does it reveal God's nature?*

- *Does it build the people listening?*

- *Is it proved to be accurate?*

We know that every revelation from God is a self-revelation of God which aims to draw us into a closer relationship with him. This means that every true Word is given for the express purpose of relating us more closely to God – and to his mind, grace, power and calling.

After listening carefully, we do not need to receive a revelation if it does not build God's people up and build them together; if it does not conform to God's nature or draw people to him; and if it is either too vague to be provable or is proved to be inaccurate.

Theological tests

We have seen repeatedly, that all prophecy must conform to the Word of God – to both the Written Word and the Personal Word. And we have also noted the biblical principle that all prophecy must bear witness to Jesus.

Passages like Deuteronomy 13:1–5; John 16:14; Acts 10:43; Romans 10:9–10; 1 Corinthians 12:3; 1 John 2:20–27; 4:1–6; 2 John 1:10 & Revelation 19:10 mean that we should also ask the following three questions about every revelation.

- *Does it agree with Scripture?*

- *Does it agree with the character of Jesus?*

- *Does it witness to Jesus – to his lordship, divinity, humanity, atoning death and resurrection, and so on?*

This does not mean that every revelation must contain a 'proof' verse and a glowing reference to Jesus before it can be accepted. Rather, it means that a revelation must be rejected if does not align with biblical principles and the revealed nature of Jesus, if it is contrary to a specific biblical injunction, and if it does not – in some way – point to him.

Moral tests

We have seen that the Old Testament identifies false prophecy by identifying false prophets. If a prophet is false, so is their prophecy – no matter how accurate or scriptural it may seem. Deuteronomy 13:1–5; 18:21–22; Jeremiah 23:9–40 & Ezekiel 12:21–14:11 suggest that false prophets have some of these distinguishing marks:

- *their predictive prophecies are inaccurate*

- *they call people after other gods*

- *their lifestyles are immoral*

- *they do not check immorality in others*

- *they call for peace with no regard to the moral and spiritual conditions required for peace*

By definition, a false prophet speaks false prophecy; and Jesus encourages us, in Matthew 7:15–20, to 'beware' of false prophets. In this passage, Jesus shows that we are not to judge by the superficial appearance of a person, but by the effect – the fruit – of their ministry and life. This means that we test prophets' lives as well as their words.

We can say that the New Testament – especially Matthew 7:15–16 & 1 John 1:6–7 – suggests three moral tests which help to identify false prophets.

- *Are they producing what Jesus considers to be good fruit?*

- *Are they walking with the Lord?*

- *Are they in good fellowship with other believers?*

No matter how astonishing a revelation, how loudly it affirms the lordship of Christ, how eloquently it quotes from the Bible, if the messenger is not walking with the Lord and other believers, and is producing bad fruit, the revelation is best ignored.

Spiritual tests

We have noted that truth is not God's truth when it is delivered with pride or self-seeking ambition. This means that we judge not only the content of a revelation, but also the life of the messenger and the 'tone' of the message.

Deuteronomy
13:1–5 ☐
18:21–22 ☐

Jeremiah
23:9–40 ☐

Ezekiel 12:21–
14:11 ☐

Matthew
7:15–20 ☐

1 John 1:6–7 ☐

As God's Word always comes to us on God's breath – on the Spirit – we need to ask ourselves whether the general tone of the revelation is consistent with the nature of the humble, self-effacing Holy Spirit.

It should be obvious that those prophets who are close to God's heart, those with greatest experience of listening to him, are in a particularly good position to test revelation. And 'prophetic agreement' is a key test of revelation.

1 Corinthians 14:29 ☐

1 Corinthians 14:29 is an important verse which suggests that genuine revelation is generally surrounded by supporting revelation and witnessed to by other prophetic men and women.

In this verse, the word 'others' in Greek is *allos*, not *heteros*. This word suggests that, in the early church, it was usually the other men and women who prophesied who judged the revelations.

If we were to follow this pattern today, it would mean that members of the congregation would not come to independent conclusions about prophetic revelations, and that leaders would not test them just because they were leaders and wanting to control proceedings. If this was what Paul meant in 1 Corinthians 14:29, he would have used a different Greek word – *heteros* – instead of *allos*.

Instead, this passage suggests that the testing of prophecies given in public worship is best left mainly to those men and women who regularly prophesy. Of course, in most churches, the 'others' will include the leaders – but they will 'test revelation' because they prophesy and not because they lead.

Judging prophecy is not a question of one person giving a 'thumbs up' or a 'thumbs down' to each prophetic message. Prophecy is so important that God wants us to treat it far more seriously than this.

In fact, judging – like prophecy – is a process which should involve:

- *congregational witness* – the Spirit is in-and-with the people, and he provides a general sense of agreement between them about God's particular Word

- *prophetic calling* – those who minister most regularly in the prophetic gift should direct the church towards God's particular Word through the gift of the discerning of spirits

- *leaders' directing* – the leaders have a governmental authority and responsibility to ensure that God's Word is recognised and applied

The gift of judging

As well as using the tests we have considered to judge revelation, the 'others' can also exercise the spiritual gift of the discerning of spirits, the gift of *diakrisis*.

This Greek word means 'thorough judging', 'thorough discerning', or – best of all – 'thorough separating'. It is used in:

- *Matthew 16:3* – to show how a meaning can be derived from a picture

- *1 Corinthians 6:5* – to establish the truth in a dispute

- *1 Corinthians 11:31* – to highlight the importance of judging

- *1 Corinthians 12:10* – as a spiritual gift

- *1 Corinthians 14:29* – to demonstrate its relevance to prophecy

We can say that *diakrisis* is the God-given spiritual gift which enables us to identify 'pure' prophecy, and to separate the divine message from the human dross in 'impure' prophecy – thus enabling us to 'hold on to the good' and 'avoid every form of evil'.

The prophetic 'judges' or 'separators' listen to all the revelations *and* to the Spirit. They bear in mind the tests that we have considered; they remember that all activity of the Spirit points to Jesus; and they appreciate that genuine biblical prophecy focuses on what God is doing, thinking, saying rather than on prescribing a human response.

The 'others' do not give a 'yes' or 'no' to each individual revelation. Instead, they separate out the human enthusiasm, cultural influences and traditional emphases, and pass on the essence of the flow of revelation.

This is not an exercise in comprehension and précis; it is a spiritual gift which operates in the same way as all spiritual gifts.

And, as with every aspect of life in the Spirit, this is extremely liberating. This sort of thorough judging – or sifting – eliminates the pastoral problems caused by rejection or fear of rebuff, and is a glowing demonstration of the church truly functioning as an inter-dependent body.

1 Corinthians
  12:10 ☐

Matthew 16:3 ☐

1 Corinthians
  6:5 ☐
  11:31 ☐

1 Corinthians
  12:10 ☐
  14:29 ☐

TESTING PERSONAL PROPHECY

As well as judging revelation which is received publicly, we also need to test revelation that we hear ourselves in our own private listening and any 'words' which are given to us personally by another believer. We need to know whether we have really heard God, or whether we have just been carried away by our own natural feelings or by the other person's spiritual or emotional pressure.

In addition to the tests that we have already considered in this chapter, there are several questions we can ask which help us to judge these personal revelations.

Test the messenger

We need to assess two matters about the man or woman who is prophesying personally to us:

- *their accountability*

We should establish whether the person is functioning properly under the care and discipline of a local church – or whether they are 'a lone ranger' or 'loose cannon'. We need to discover who corrects them, and whether they submit to this – or whether, in reality, they are unaccountable.

- *their life-style*

We should also check their 'fruit'. This includes their character, their doctrine and the results of their ministry. We need to discover whether they are Christ-like in their life and ministry, whether they are biblical in their beliefs, and whether God's kingdom is being built through them.

Even though a prophecy may be accurate, we should reject it if the messenger fails the biblical tests. We should remember that:

- *false prophets were rejected by Jesus, even though they apparently prophesied as effectively as they cast out demons* – Matthew 7:15–23

- *Caiaphas prophesied accurately, even though he was not a follower of Christ* – John 11:45

Matthew
7:15–23 ☐

John 11:45 ☐

- *Balaam used pagan means of divination as well as prophesying in the name of the Lord, so God overthrew his pronouncements and turned his curse into a blessing for Israel – Numbers 22–24*

Numbers 22–24 ☐

Test the message

There are a whole series of practical questions that we can consider about each personal prophesy. Some of them may be more relevant for testing those revelations that we hear in our own private listening, and others may be more relevant for testing those revelations which others pass on to us.

The most important point to remember is that we should *always* test *every* message thoroughly.

- *is the revelation factual?*

If someone is speaking by the Spirit, their words will be accurate: the signs they announce will happen, their predictions will come to pass.

We should realise, however, that prophecy is not verbally inspired in the same way as Scripture. The Spirit may be giving a core revelation or 'essence', but human elements may be distorting it.

We also need to remember that accuracy is not a proof of genuineness. Supernatural facts do not, on their own, constitute a prophecy, for they may have come from a demonic source.

- *is it biblical?*

If the message contains false doctrine, it cannot have come from the Holy Spirit for every prophecy must submit completely to Scripture.

- *is it confirmed and confirming?*

If God is truly speaking, we can expect that he will confirm his Word through several means and sources. We see this principle in Matthew 18:19–20; Acts 13:2 & 1 Corinthians 13:1.

Matthew 18:19–20 ☐

Acts 13:2 ☐

1 Corinthians 13:1 ☐

- *does the revelation come with the witness of the Spirit?*

The Holy Spirit bears witness to true words of prophecy, and because he is in-and-with us we can expect him to provide us with his inner seal to genuine revelations.

Of course, we must be sure that we do not confuse the Spirit's witness with a human reaction – especially when a prophecy challenges a pre-conceived idea, a religious tradition or a cultural standard!

We have seen that one way the Spirit does this is through his 'fruit'. We can ask ourselves whether the message is consistent with his love, joy, peace, patience, gentleness, and so on.

- *does it make no attempt to by-pass our responsibility to make decisions?*

Genuine prophecy points to what God is doing, and calls us to fall in step with him. It may point us to God's particular will, it may even challenge us to obey his will – but it does not insist that we obey unthinkingly, without checking the revelation. Every revelation should be checked with wise counsellors and godly, mature leaders.

- *does it avoid areas which are excessively personal?*

We must be very wary of messages from people who insist that God has told them who we should or should not marry, what colour we should paint our homes, what type of car we should buy, and so on.

- *is the revelation consistent with God's counsel for our lives?*

For the most part, personal prophecy should confirm things which God has already been saying. He may give us new information through a personal prophecy, but this will be in line with what we know of God's over-all plan for our lives.

We should be careful if we receive something which does not fit with what we know. We should not reject the revelation outright, but we should set it aside and ask the Lord to clarify the situation.

- *does it claim too high a level of inspiration or authority?*

We have seen that not all prophecies carry the same level of inspiration. A personal message will often be nothing more than inspired comfort or encouragement, but it may – at times – be a major word of direction, correction or prediction.

God almost always entrusts such 'major' words to experienced and mature prophetic people. Most mistakes occur when people begin to prophesy outside the 'proportion of their faith' or the gift that God has given them. We must be especially careful with any words which apparently determine some aspect of our futures.

Test everything

It is difficult to overstate the importance of this chapter about judging revelation. Any emphasis on listening to God and prophetic speaking must include a biblical understanding of testing revelation.

This is never an easy area, and we need to approach it with great humility. But when we listen without testing, or prophesy without judging, we open the door to error, unhelpful emotions, human pressure, and demonic distractions.

PART NINE

developing prophetic listening

It is a tragedy that, despite all the conferences, books and sermons of recent years, there still does not seem to be a recognised place for regular prophecy in most sections of the church. Few congregations make room for prophecy, and treat it with holy respect.

Many leaders do not believe that prophetic listening and revelation are God's way of communicating today. Even in some pentecostal and charismatic churches, there is a paralysing fear of false prophets, an acceptance of superficial prophecy, and confusion about the judgement of prophecy.

We should grasp that Satan is firmly opposed to prophecy, and is determined to do his utmost to defame it and tempt believers to ignore it. He has good grounds for his opposition, because prophecy is so valuable to the church.

As we have seen, God speaks through prophecy. He uses it to manifest his presence, to bring edification, encouragement and comfort to believers, and to bring conviction to those who are not yet saved.

Through prophecy, God reveals his character, directs the actions of his people, warns them to escape from trouble, prepares them to meet difficulties, and points to those whom he wants in his service at home and overseas.

Through prophecy, we can know the particular Word of God and the immediate will of God, and we can emulate Jesus' resolution to do only what he hears and sees the Father doing.

It is vital, therefore, that we establish a clearly accepted and recognised role for prophets and prophecy in the church today, and that we know how to develop prophetic listening and living through-out every congregation.

There are several different things that both leaders and ordinary believers can do to develop prophetic listening to God.

THE LEADERS

Christian believers need to be confident that their leaders will treat their prophesying seriously, and will not regard it as a harmless eccentricity. The prophetic ministry rarely develops in churches whose leaders think that they should allow someone 'to say their little piece', but can then quietly ignore what is said.

Public response

Leaders should make a public response to prophesying. In fact, they should not admit prophecy without also admitting a means of dealing with it.

At the moment, some ministers do not make room for prophecy because they fear the possibility of unhelpful pressure by a strong-minded individual. If someone brings a revelation, it tends to be received with an embarrassed silence – and then quickly forgotten.

But the biblical principle of 'judging' a flow of prophecies to reveal the essence of God's Word eliminates the pastoral problems of human pressure and personal rejection.

Quite simply, 1 Thessalonians 5:20 makes it plain that no leader should ever ignore prophecy. In every church tradition, it is possible to establish an appropriate 'decently and orderly' pattern for the manifestation of spiritual gifts. The leaders should ensure that this pattern is known and followed, that they allow room for blunders and failures – and that they acknowledge these inevitable slips with a smile.

We know that we can learn more from mistakes than from doing nothing, and that we cannot reach maturity without passing through an immature phase. These truths apply to prophecy as much as to every other aspect of our physical and spiritual lives.

Public direction

Most people, especially visitors, find it helpful when ministers provide some sort of commentary or explanation about spiritual gifts, and when they guide and direct people about the procedure which is followed in that congregation.

Leaders should try to ensure that there is a biblical *taxis* – order and orderliness – to their services, and should make room for 'all things', without permitting an anarchic or chaotic free-for-all.

As all revelation is subject to God's Written Word, the leaders must know Scripture and be able both to defend sound doctrine and to expose false doctrine.

They should also assess the characters of the people prophesying – to prevent infiltration by false prophets – without forgetting the Numbers 22:28–30 principle. If God can speak in this way, he can surely speak through the most ancient, or young, or immature, or uneducated, or unprepossessing believers.

Public encouragement

Ephesians 4:11–12 teaches that pastors have the primary responsibility of equipping believers for the tasks of ministry and church-building. As prophecy is a fundamental part of church edification, pastors and teachers should actively help 'the saints' to prophesy.

Many believers need constant encouragement to trust the thoughts that God gives them; others need direction to help them move from

1 Thessalonians 5:20 ☐

Numbers 22:28–30 ☐

Ephesians 4:11–12 ☐

superficial platitudes to specific prophecy; and some need guidance on how and when to stop speaking.

Finally, if prophetic listening and living is to develop in a church, the leaders must set an example in the public *zelotes* for prophecy. If they long for prophecy, if they make listening their personal priority, then the people will themselves begin to 'hear' God 'speak' more clearly.

But if the leaders are thought to be against prophecy – or at least to be rather suspicious – it is unlikely whether the people will bother to listen to God and take his prophetic Word seriously.

THE PEOPLE

Listening to God is listening to his Word. If we yearn to hear God 'speak', we must saturate ourselves in his Written Word and live close to his Personal Word – there are no short-cuts or instant solutions which alleviate our need for a disciplined lifestyle.

Devour the Bible

Prophetic inspiration comes through our exposure to the Word and our openness to the Spirit.

- *We need to keep on devouring the Bible to hear most of God's thoughts.*

- *We need to read it regularly, thoroughly, carefully – with spiritual 'ears' which are alert for God's way of underlining his rhema Word to us.*

- *We need to read every part of the Scriptures – Old and New, Leviticus and Luke, Amos and Acts, Habakkuk and Hebrews, and so on.*

- *And we need to remember the truths of 1 Thessalonians 2:13 and 1 Corinthians 2:14. The Spirit who originated the Scriptures must also make them clear to us, for the truths they contain are spiritually, not intellectually, discerned.*

1 Thessalonians
    2:13 ☐

1 Corinthians
    2:14 ☐

When we do this, we must consciously align ourselves with the teaching of the Bible, for understanding without gospel obedience is always sinful. God does not speak his Word just to teach us facts about him; he gives us his Word essentially so that we may know *him* – personally, intimately, directly and joyfully.

As we see in *Knowing the Father*, gospel obedience is enabled obedience rather than fleshly self effort: it is only through the work of the Spirit that the Word accomplishes its purposes in human lives.

This illustrates the importance of both an intimate openness to the Holy Spirit *and* a close acquaintance with the Written Word.

Zealous for prophecy

Like the leaders, every believer should follow the thrice-repeated injunction of 1 Corinthians 14. We must be zealous for the gift of prophecy to be established in our church, in all churches.

Without a hint of spiritual ambition, we should offer ourselves to God as humble servants who are willing to act in obedience to the prompting of his Spirit. All God needs is an ear and a mouth, and we should volunteer to be one of his servant messengers – who speak only what he says, both to the world and to the church.

Expect God to speak

When we start to become serious about prophetic listening and living, we must expect God to 'speak' to us, to summon us into his presence, to whisper his thoughts in our 'ears', to place his 'burden' on our 'shoulders', and so on.

Many people find it helpful to use a notebook to record the dreams, thoughts and words which they think may be God's Word for them. Over a period of time, this habit can help us to identify the persistent whispers which we tend to overlook.

If God seems to suggest something which is not for us personally, we should ask him whether this thought is a word which should be passed on to another person or group of people.

When we suspect that God has spoken a word to us which we should pass on, we must allow ourselves to be directed by him as to the place, time and person. We must trust ourselves completely to the Spirit – who will prompt us as to where, when, who and what.

Identify fears

Most believers are rightly rather apprehensive about speaking God's Word to another person. When this is the case, it is good to identify the cause of the fear so that we can ask God to deal with it.

We should ask ourselves whether, for example, we are afraid of:

- *what others will think?*

- *being unable to finish the prophecy?*

- *saying something silly?*

- *appearing foolish?*

In fact, we should always be more afraid of what God thinks if we disobey him by failing to speak, than of what others will say if obey him and speak.

We must grasp that we can develop by learning from our errors and failings, but that we learn nothing by remaining silent when God has directed us to speak.

We must empathise with other believers who are learning to listen to God and speak prophetically, and put up with their stumbling attempts.

And we must get on with our prophetic listening and living – so that the 'voice' of God can be heard with ever-increasing clarity, authority and power in that part of the world where we have been placed.

PROPHETIC INTERCESSION

As well as developing prophetic listening in these distinctive ways, leaders and ordinary believers both need to develop their listening through prophetic intercession. Although we should aim to develop a listening life which is *constantly* alert for God's voice, we can only build such an attentive life on the foundation of listening prayer.

We know that God wants us to draw close to him so that he can reveal his deepest thoughts to us. And he does this through prayer.

Prayer has to do with everything that we are not in and of ourselves, but many of us are taken up with our own concerns and ideas. Even when we pray, personal matters cloud our minds to God's will and to *his* concerns and burdens.

When we approach God in prayer, we should be more eager to receive his Word than to pass on our worries – we should draw near to him with empty hands and an open spirit.

We consider intercession in some detail in *Effective Prayer* and note that we need to receive God's direction for our intercession. All the great intercessors of the Bible were Spirit-anointed prophets, and they all followed a strict order in their intercession:

1. *in prayer, they entered God's presence*

2. *they quietly and patiently listened for God's revelation*

3. *they spoke that revelation back to God in intercessory prayer*

4. *they announced the revelation to the relevant people*

We can say that prophetic intercession is revelation praying, and is – for most people – the way into a life of listening prophetically to God.

True biblical intercession is not a recital of the needs of our relations, or a working through a list of our requirements. Instead, genuine, scriptural, prophetic intercession always begins with quiet, persistent waiting for a revelation of the heart of God.

As we have seen, the Old Testament prophets received:

• *a vision from God – they saw what he saw*

• *a burden from God – they felt what he felt*

• *a Word from God – they heard what he said*

It is the same today: our biblical intercession begins when we receive a revelation from God – and this does *not* usually explode into our senses in a way which overpowers our minds and demands our immediate attention.

Like Elijah in 1 Kings 19:9–18, we need to learn that God's voice is rarely like a hurricane, an earthquake or a raging fire – it is more

1 Kings 19:9–18 ☐

commonly like a light murmuring sound which can be heard only by those who are listening intently.

Prophetic revelation naturally leads to prophetic intercession, and many revelations are given for the purpose of directing and encouraging intercession. Although we are God's servant messengers, we should not be emotionally separated from our message; instead, we are genuine partners in the prophetic message who intercede with God about our message, praying that his purposes are accomplished.

Numbers 14:13–19 ☐

We see this listening→revelation→intercession progression particularly clearly in Numbers 14:13–19, where Moses intercedes in response to the revelation that God is ready to destroy his people.

In this passage, three factors shape Moses' prophetic intercession:

God's reputation

Moses knew that God's reputation was at stake. If the people were destroyed, the surrounding pagan nations would think that *Yahweh* was unable to keep his promise.

Moses was not trying to strike a bargain with God; he had a real concern for God's name and reputation. He had seen God's glory and now he was jealous for it. The revelation of God's intention caused him to intercede with God to preserve God's reputation.

God's character

Exodus 33:12– 34:8 ☐

Because of his intimate relationship with God, which we see in Exodus 33:12–34:8, Moses knew that God was characterised by mercy and forgiveness. His intercession was virtually, 'God remember your self-revelation on Sinai, forgive the people!'

Moses was not trying to manipulate God, he was interceding according to the Word he had already received about God's character.

God's people

Moses had a deep concern for the people of God, and was fully identified with them. He loved them and did not want them to be destroyed, so he interceded because he cared for this group of people.

Like Moses, our intercessions are often shaped and prompted by our compassion and concern for people – but this is not enough. The revelation which is the fruit of our listening must also determine our praying – as should our knowledge and love of God.

THE LISTENING LIFE

Once we have learnt to listen to God in prayer, we need to move on to recognise his 'voice' in a host of other ways – as well as continuing to listen to him in prayer.

God is the Great Communicator who speaks to us today both personally and directly. When we have developed a 'prayer-life' which is shaped more around listening than making requests, we can go on to listen for God's voice in all the ways that we have seen him 'speaking' in the Scriptures to his people.

The Bible

Passages like 1 Corinthians 10:11; 2 Timothy 3:16–17 & Hebrews 4:12–13 remind us of the living power and value of the Written Word.

1 Corinthians 10:11 ☐

2 Timothy 3:16–17 ☐

Hebrews 4:12–13 ☐

God speaks to us in our spirits through the Bible by drawing our attention to a particular verse, character or incident. Sometimes, he does this as we read the Scriptures for ourselves, as we listen to them read publicly, or as we hear them expounded by a teacher; at other times he prompts us to remember a phrase or passage that we have read or heard in the past.

It is imperative that we saturate ourselves in the Word – by personal reading, study, meditation and memorisation; by listening to biblical preaching and teaching; and by using teaching books and other aids.

The natural world

Genesis 9:12–17; Psalm 19:1–6; Proverbs 6:6–8; Matthew 6:25–30 and Romans 1:18–20 illustrate the truth that God communicates with us through his creation and the natural world.

Genesis 9:12–17 ☐

Psalm 19:1–6 ☐

Proverbs 6:6–8 ☐

Matthew 6:25–30 ☐

Romans 1:18–20 ☐

At times, God 'speaks' to us in our spirits when we notice the detail in a tiny aspect of creation, or when we are awed by the size and magnificent complexity of a great vista, or when we are just spending time in his company enjoying his handiwork.

Many of us lead such busy lives today that we spend little time 'walking with God in the garden'. If developing a listening life is our sincere aim, we will need to create spaces in our lives when we are alone with God – not just to pray, but also to enjoy him and his creation.

God does want to be involved with us in every aspect of our lives; but he also wants us to share with him in *his* life and to appreciate *his* activities.

Events and circumstances

We have seen that God communicates through national events and personal circumstances. This is not the only way that he 'speaks', and we must receive the Spirit's wisdom to interpret events accurately, but God does speak to us in our spirits through the detail of our lives – even, as James 5:14–15 shows, through sickness.

> James 5:14–15 □

God uses and allows our circumstances, for example:

- *to discipline us* – Hebrews 12:3–11

> Hebrews 12:3–11 □

- *to humble and test us* – Deuteronomy 8:2–5

> Deuteronomy 8:2–5 □

- *to manifest his power and love* – Exodus 14:30–31

> Exodus 14:30–31 □

Everything that happens to us, and to our nation, is part of God's 'permissive' will; it is 'allowed' by him, even if it is not necessarily his 'perfect' will. This means that, as in Jeremiah 9:12–16, we often need a prophetic interpretation of events to understand what God is saying *through* our circumstances.

> Jeremiah 9:12–16 □

Impressions

We know that the Holy Spirit has access to the inner recesses of our hearts and minds. As a result, he can communicate directly with our human spirits in a 'trans-rational' manner through holy 'impressions'. These often come, for example, through:

- *thoughts*

- *words*

- *ideas*

- *pictures*

- *physical sensations*

- *an inner voice*

- *prophetic speech*

- *tongues*

- *interpretation*

- *the gift of prophecy*

Some believers seem to think that these trans-rational impressions are God's 'normal' way of communicating today. But we need to recognise that they are merely one of many ways, and that they are not 'superior' or 'more spiritual' to any other way.

When God does speak to us in this way, we need to take care to ensure that his Word is tested and is not misunderstood.

Dreams and vision

The Scriptures make it plain that God sometimes communicates with his people through dreams by night and visions by day.

We see this throughout the Old Testament, at Jesus' nativity, at his death, and at important stages in the development of the early church, for example: Genesis 15:1; 20:3–7; 28:12–15; 37:5–11; 40:8–19; 41:1–36; Numbers 12:6–8; Deuteronomy 13:1–5; 1 Samuel 3:9–15; Ezekiel 1:1–3:15; Daniel 1:17; 2:1–45; 5:11–12; Joel 2:28; Matthew 1:20–21; 2:12–13, 19–23; 27:19; Acts 9:10–16; 10:3–6; 11:5–10; 16:9–10; 18:9–10; 2 Corinthians 12:1–4 and Revelation 1:10.

This does not mean that all our dreams always contain messages from God, rather that – at times – he draws our attention to his Word through a dream or vision.

We should not ignore our dreams, but we do not need to try to remember and understand them all.

Genesis 15:1 ☐
20:3–7 ☐
28:12–15 ☐
37:5–11 ☐
40:8–19 ☐
41:1–36 ☐
Numbers 12:6–8 ☐
Deuteronomy
13:1–5 ☐

1 Samuel 3:9–15 ☐
Ezekiel 1:1–3:15 ☐
Daniel 1:17 ☐
2:1–45 ☐
5:11–12 ☐
Joel 2:28 ☐
Matthew
1:20–21 ☐
2:12–13 ☐
2:19–23 ☐
27:19 ☐
Acts 9:10–16 ☐
10:3–6 ☐
11:5–10 ☐
16:9–10 ☐
18:9–10 ☐
2 Corinthians
12:1–4 ☐
Revelation 1:10 ☐

As we build a listening life on listening prayer, so we will come to recognise God's way of highlighting aspects of our lives – including our subconscious side – to reveal his *rhema* Word.

An audible voice

We have often noted that God rarely speaks with an audible voice which we hear with our physical ears. We must recognise, however, that there are occasional rare occurrences – as in Exodus 3:4–4:17 and 1 Samuel 3:4–14 – when God does speak audibly.

Exodus 3:4–4:17 ☐
1 Samuel 3:4–14 ☐

THE LISTENING PROCESS

In *Living Faith*, we see that it is easier to focus on one part of a process than to appreciate the full process: this common error also applies to prophecy. For example, many sections of the church think about prophecy essentially in terms of speaking, while – in this book – we have concentrated more on the listening foundation.

We must remember, however, that prophecy is a complete process which involves:

- *a summons into the presence of God*

- *an intimate relationship with him*

- *persistent, careful listening*

- *receiving his Word through the Spirit*

- *judging or separating the Word*

- *passing on God's Word to the appropriate person or group*

Prophecy involves all these stages, and the whole process may take a considerable time – it is rarely one quick event!

We have also seen that the whole church is called to be zealous for prophecy, and that several people are involved in the judging of prophecy. The prophetic process is rarely an individual activity, it normally involves the church: we need to learn to listen together as well as on our own, to judge each other's revelations, to submit our revelations to others for judging, and – most importantly – to trust the tested revelations of others.

As we go on to live a listening life, we will often need to remind ourselves about the full process, and to check that we are paying attention to every part. In summary, we need to:

1. *listen to God within the context of an intimate personal relationship, serving partnership, and Spirit-directed worship*

2. *understand that he speaks to us essentially to reveal himself to us – his revelation always enhances his relationship with us*

3. *note what God shows through whatever means he chooses to use*

4. *interpret the revelation carefully, with the help of the Spirit's wisdom and insight, so that we do not misunderstand the meaning and purpose of the message*

5. *judge, test, weigh, discern, separate and test the revelation biblically, making sure that it is in line with scripture, sanctified common sense, other revelations, and so on*

6. *apply it wisely and handle it gently, ensuring that we learn from God how he means it to be applied, who he wants us to give it to, when it should be passed on, who should speak it, and so on*

7. *double-check our motivation in prophesying, ensuring that we are not seeking to draw attention to ourselves and that we want to build the church and not condemn those who irritate us*

8. *give the Word with grace and gentleness*

9. *eagerly receive and obey any tested revelation for ourselves*

FIRST STEPS IN PROPHETIC LISTENING AND LIVING

We have learnt that – since Pentecost – every Spirit-filled Christian can prophesy, and that the man or woman with a prophetic ministry is simply the one who prophesies most frequently.

We urgently need a truly prophetic church, and we need men and women with the ministry of prophet in every local church. God will use anybody who is willing to seek his face, to seek his gifts and to be bold enough to give it a try.

Some believers are unsure what to do when they first start to listen seriously to God: the following practical suggestions can help believers to take their first tentative steps towards a life of prophetic listening.

- *remind ourselves that God's great desire is to reveal himself, his will and his Word to all his children – he is speaking and he wants us to know his voice*

- *bind the enemy to stop him putting distracting voices and thoughts in our minds – we consider this in 'Ministry in the Spirit'*

- *blot out all other thoughts*

- *read a passage of Scripture to help us focus on God*

- *pray briefly in tongues – this strengthens our spirits and prepares them to receive revelation*

- *be open and receptive to God, and listen for his thoughts, promptings and suggestions*

- *note whatever comes into out spirits*

- *check and test these thoughts*

- *ask God for clarity and confirmation*

- *be patient, take time*

- *share the revelation with a more experienced discipline, and ask them to test it for you*

- *be willing to receive correction and confirmation*

- *act on the revelation – under the clear directing of the Spirit*

Here I am. Send me

Mark 4:14–20 □

Hebrews 4:2 □

James 1:22 □

Passages like Mark 4:14–20; Hebrews 4:2 and James 1:22 emphasise the truth that listening to God is not enough: we must also act on the words that we hear. Quite simply, we deceive ourselves when we listen without acting.

The Apostle Paul gave Timothy some important advice about this which is relevant to us:

- *use the word that God has given you, and do battle with it –* 1 Timothy 1:18

- *do not neglect the gift that God has imparted to you –* 1 Timothy 4:14

- *stir up the prophetic message in you: keep it alive –* 2 Timothy 1:1–7

Like Timothy, we must hold on to the words we hear, work out what God is saying to us, and then act on them with wisdom – in full dependence on the Holy Spirit and in keeping with every other Christian discipline, with prayer, for example, the Scriptures and Christian fellowship.

Isaiah 6:5 describes Isaiah's humble response to God's prophetic message. Like him, we do not volunteer to be one of God's prophetic servants out of pride or ambition, instead we come knowing the reality of our flawed lives – and knowing that our faults and inadequacies do not disqualify us. In fact, in as much as our weaknesses cause us to depend on the Holy Spirit, they are positive assets.

Isaiah 6:6–8 then reports how God cleansed Isaiah, and then asked him question which he still puts to us: 'Whom shall I send? And who will go for us?' May Isaiah's response be ours.

As we draw near to God, aware of our sins and shortcomings, we can be certain that he desires to cleanse and equip us – and that he has a unique commission which only we can fulfil. When we learn to listen personally to him – and to respond with gospel obedience – we will be drawn deeper into his life, and will see him work more creatively and powerfully in the lives of the hurting people around us.

ACTIVITIES for individuals and small groups

prophetic listening

List the most important reasons for listening to God.

....

....

....

....

....

....

How does the devil try to prevent you from listening to God?

....

....

....

....

What does the phrase 'prophetic listening' mean?

....

....

Why do you listen to God?

....

....

When do you listen to him?

....

....

How do you listen to him?

....

....

....

APPRECIATING THE LISTENING PROCESS

How can you develop a deeper sense of awe at the thought of the living, loving God actually communicating with you?

....

....

....

How does your listening affect God?

....

....

....

What is the primary purpose of all revelation?

....

How does 'guidance' reveal something about God himself?

....

....

....

In the last few months, which revelations have you disobeyed? Why was this?

....

....

....

Which would you prefer: great wealth, high office, miraculous powers, encyclopaedic knowledge or a hearing heart?

....

Which of these does God want to develop in your life?

....

Why is this so important to him?

....

....

the communicating god

How does the Bible stress that God communicates with the world that he has made?

....

....

How does the Bible introduce God?

....

....

What does Isaiah 44:6 teach about God?

....

....

....

Why does God not communicate with us through inanimate objects?

....

....

Where are you closest to God?

....

....

Why do some people think that statues, special buildings, open spaces, etc., help them to hear God more clearly?

....

....

How could you help someone who believed that a religious trinket enabled them to hear God better?

....

....

....

....

GOD IS ACTIVE

What does God's Genesis 12:3 promise to Abram reveal about God?

....

....

....

What did the events of the exodus reveal to Israel about God's character?

....

....

....

Which personal problems and social pressures cause you to struggle with God's promises?

....

....

....

How do the Old Testament prophets respond to these sorts of struggles?

....

....

....

....

*What do these passages reveal about God? Psalm 47; Isaiah 44:1–20; 45:1–4; 47:1–15; 49:6 &
Amos 1:3–2:5.*

....

....

How have you encountered the active, speaking God in a terrible personal tragedy?

....

....

....

....

GOD IS PERSONAL

Although the Old Testament concentrates on the way that God communicates with Israel, and shows how he communicates with them as a nation, it is wrong to imagine that God deals with people only in large numbers.

Which Old Testament stories reveal God's personal concern for individual Jews and pagans?

....

....

....

What do these passages teach about the personal way that God relates to people? Exodus 4:22; Isaiah 1:2; 49:15; 66:13; Jeremiah 31:32; Ezekiel 16:3–8; Hosea 2:14–23 & 11:4.

....

....

....

GOD IS HIDDEN

Many people do not see amazing events like the exodus, or have unusual experiences like Moses and Isaiah; they wonder whether the Bible's teaching about God is still relevant.

It was the same, however, in Old Testament days, for their lives were just as affected by evil and suffering as ours our today. There are times when God seems far from powerful and active, and when the realities of life seem inconsistent with God's past deeds.

How did these people struggle with God's hiddenness?

Abraham ....

....

Moses ....

....

Elijah ....

....

Jeremiah ....

....

REVELATION PRINCIPLES

What are the two main biblical assumptions about God which determine the way that he communicates with people?

1. ....

2. ....

What does God's essential graciousness mean in terms of revelation?

....

....

....

How should God's grace effect the way that you listen to God?

....

....

....

What is the biblical relationship between God's speaking and his acting?

....

....

....

How do we see the God-who-speaks-to-create working in creation?

....

....

How do we see the God-who-speaks-to-create working through prophecy?

....

....

What does this mean for your listening to God?

....

....

....

....

the word of god

What do these passages teach about the way that God communicates with us?

Psalm 19:1–6 ....

Jeremiah 9:12–16 ....

Romans 2:14–15 ....

1 Thessalonians 5:20 ....

2 Timothy 3:16–17 ....

Hebrews 1:1–3 ....

What is God's primary reason for speaking to us through these means?

....

What is the general scriptural name for God's means of communication?

....

What does the Hebrew word 'dabar' literally mean? And to what does it point?

....

....

Why does God want you to listen to his Word?

....

....

Why are the Scriptures the essential written form of the Word, not the totality of the Word?

....

....

What is the central purpose of the Bible – the Written Word?

....

What helpful attitudes follow on from a right thinking about the full Word?

....

....

....

LOGOS & RHEMA

What is the difference between 'logos' and 'rhema'?

....

....

....

God has supremely revealed himself to humanity through Jesus and through the Bible. We can therefore think of Jesus as God's 'Personal Word' and the Bible as God's 'Written Word'. This is why they are both identified as God's 'logos'.

How should the realisation that Jesus is 'the Word of God' affect our listening to God?

....

....

....

What did the expression 'the Word' mean in the early church?

....

....

....

With what must every 'rhema' word agree?

....

....

....

What does a 'rhema' word actually do?

....

....

In the last few months, what 'rhema' words has God spoken to you?

....

....

....

....

THE WORD OF GOD

*What do these passages teach about the relationship between God's Word and God's breath –
the Holy Spirit? Psalm 33:6; 2 Timothy 3:16–17; 2 Peter 1:19–21.*

....

....

....

....

Why must the Word always achieve its purpose?

....

....

What do these passages show the God 'who-speaks-to-act' achieving through the Word?

Psalm 17:4 ....

Psalm 19:11 ....

Psalm 107:20 ....

Psalm 119:105 ....

John 5:24 ....

Romans 10:17 ....

Ephesians 5:25–27 ....

Ephesians 6:17 ....

James 1:18 ....

1 Peter 2:1–2 ....

There are many situations when the Bible does not distinguish between different options, and
we need the Spirit to speak to us specifically – in more detail than is possible in the Bible.

*What is the most recent way that God has guided you, first generally through the Scriptures, and
then very specifically by the Spirit?*

....

....

....

the will of god

Gospel obedience is 'enabled' obedience, not 'required' obedience. The Father does not make impossible demands and then stand back to watch us fail; instead, he gives us the Son and the Spirit by whom he enables us to obey him. And it is personal obedience to 'Abba', not legal obedience to a code of principles and regulations.

What does Romans 12:1–2 teach about gospel obedience?

....

....

....

What does John 5:1–15 teach about gospel obedience?

....

....

....

What does Acts 16:6–10 teach about gospel obedience?

....

....

Is gospel obedience a grateful human response to God's grace, or an absolute requirement for his grace? Why is this?

....

....

....

Does God speak to us because we ask him? Or do we ask him to speak because we know that it is his will to speak to us? Why is this? What difference does this make?

....

....

....

....

....

UNDERSTANDING GOD'S WILL

Because God is spiritual, he rarely reveals his Word audibly. Instead, he normally 'speaks' by the Spirit in a variety of ways that we discern by faith in our spirits. As well as breathing his Word to us through the Bible, he also reveals his will to our spirits in many other ways.

For each of the following means of guidance, suggest one scriptural example, and one example from your own experience.

Circumstances ....
....
....
....
....

Godly thinking ....
....
....
....

The Spirit's witness ....
....
....
....

A 'rhema' word ....
....
....
....

Godly desires ....
....
....
....

Dreams & visions ....

....

....

....

Spiritual gifts ....

....

....

....

The fruit of the Spirit ....

....

....

....

Godly counsel ....

....

....

....

How does God generally confirm his revelation of his will?

....

....

Why does God act in this way? What has it to do with God himself?

....

....

....

What is your experience of this?

....

....

....

....

old testament prophetic listening

What is a good definition of general Christian prophecy?

....

....

How were prophets described in the Old Testament?

....

....

What do the Hebrew words 'nabi', 'roeh' & 'hozeh' reveal about the prophetic calling?

....

....

....

What do these passages teach about prophetic revelation? 1 Samuel 3:7; Isaiah 50:4–5; Amos 3:7; Daniel 9:23; 10:11; John 13:21–26

....

....

....

....

....

....

What was the primary purpose of the Old Testament prophetic calling?

....

....

....

What was the secondary purpose of the prophetic calling?

....

....

....

THE PROPHETIC FUNCTION

After listening, the main function of the prophets was to speak God's words: they had to act on what they heard. Their prophetic words can be loosely classified in five broad areas.

What do the following passages teach about the prophetic message?

Isaiah 2:2–5; Amos 5; Zephaniah 1:14 – 2:3; Hosea 5

....

....

....

....

Leviticus 19:9–18; Deuteronomy 23:15–25; 2 Chronicles 28:9–15; Amos 2:6–7; 4:1–3; 8:4–8

....

....

....

....

Deuteronomy 18:15, 22; 1 Kings 11:29–39; 14:1–18; Isaiah 1:7–9; 7:14; 41:21–23; 45:20–22

....

....

....

....

Genesis 20; Numbers 12; 1 Kings 13; 17:7–24; 2 Kings 4:8–37; 20:1–11; Jeremiah 38:14–28

....

....

....

....

Genesis 20:7; Exodus 18:19; Numbers 27:5; 1 Kings 13:6; 2 Kings 19:4; Zechariah 7:1–3

....

....

....

PROPHETIC INSPIRATION

The Old Testament prophets were inspired in four main ways. What do the following passages teach about prophetic inspiration? What is your experience of each type of inspiration?

Isaiah 6:1–10; Ezekiel 1:1–3; Jeremiah 1:11; 18:1–4; 24; Amos 3:8; 7:7 Zechariah 1:1, 7

....

....

....

....

Habakkuk 1:1; Jeremiah 23:33–40

....

....

....

....

Numbers 11:29; 1 Samuel 10; 19:18–24; Micah 3:8; Joel 2:28

....

....

....

....

Numbers 12:6; Isaiah 6; Ezekiel 12:8; Daniel 7:1; 9:21; Zechariah 1:8–9

....

....

....

....

Why does the way that the prophets speak differ from prophet to prophet? Why do they prophesy in so many different styles?

....

....

....

new testament prophetic listening

Why did so many people in Jesus' day recognise that he was a prophet?

....

....

What do these passages teach about Jesus' prophetic ministry?

John 1:18; Matthew 11:27 ....

....

John 4:34; 5:19, 30; 6:38; 7:28–29; 8:28–29; 10:18 ....

....

....

John 12:49–50; 14:10 ....

....

John 9:17; Acts 10:34–48 ....

....

....

Matthew 3:1–12; Mark 1:1–8; Luke 3:1–18; John 1:19–34; Acts 1:1–5 ....

....

....

Mark 1:35; Luke 5:16; 6:12; 9:18, 28–29; 22:41; 23:34; 24:30; Romans 8:34; Hebrews 7:25

....

....

Matthew 15:32; 20:34; 23:23; Luke 7:13; 10:33; John 8:1–12 ....

....

....

Matthew 11:20–24; Luke 21:20–28; John 21:15–19 ....

....

....

PROPHECY IN THE EARLY CHURCH

What are the key differences between prophecy before and after Pentecost?

....

....

....

The book of Acts records how the risen Christ directed the early church through prophetic revelation and insights. How have you been directed in a similar way?

....

....

....

....

....

....

What are the implications for your church of Acts 2:18? ....

....

....

....

What are the implications for you of Revelation 19:10?

....

....

....

How does personal and congregational prophecy relate to Scripture?

....

....

....

....

....

PROPHETS IN THE EARLY CHURCH

How did people become prophets in the early church?

....

....

....

What do these verses teach about the ministry of prophets?

Ephesians 4:7–16 ....

....

Ephesians 3:5 ....

....

Acts 13:1–3 ....

....

Acts 21:10–14 ....

....

Acts 11:27–30 ....

....

1 Timothy 1:18; 4:14; 2 Timothy 1:6 ....

....

What is your experience of this sort of biblical prophetic ministry?

....

....

....

What is God saying to you about the prophetic ministry?

....

....

....

....

THE GIFT OF PROPHECY

How does the gift of prophecy differ from the ministry of prophets?

....

....

....

....

How does the gift of prophecy relate to general prophecy?

....

....

....

....

What does the context of 1 Corinthians 12–14 suggest about the gift of prophecy?

....

....

How does this gift function in your church at the moment?

....

....

....

....

....

What changes would need to be made to bring this more into line with 1 Corinthians 14?

....

....

....

....

....

....

prophetic listening today

What different stages are involved in the prophetic process? ....

....

Which of these stages do you focus too much upon, and which do you need to give more time?

....

....

What is the trinitarian base of prophetic listening?

....

....

How does prophecy relate to Scripture?

....

....

....

What does 1 Thessalonians 5:19–21 teach about prophecy?

....

....

How does your church work out its general prophetic function in its local community?

....

....

....

What is God saying about your personal, general prophetic role in the church and the world?

....

....

....

....

....

THE PROPHETIC GIFT

According to the Bible, what are the main purposes of the prophetic gift?

....

....

When should you expect God to give this gift to you?

....

....

1 Corinthians 14:26 suggests that we should come to public worship both prepared to contribute and with a prepared contribution. How does this relate to your life?

....

....

....

What prevents you from manifesting this gift more than you do?

....

....

....

What temptations do you face to manufacture this gift or to prophecy in an uncontrolled way?

....

....

....

How can you become more 'zealous' for this gift?

....

....

....

How do you submit your prophetic words for judging and scrutiny?

....

....

....

THE PROPHETIC MINISTRY

Why do we need prophets today?

....

....

....

....

How does the prophets' ministry from the Word differ from, and complement, the ministry of pastors and teachers?

....

....

....

....

What sort of revelation can prophets bring to individual people?

....

....

....

What sort of revelation can they bring to the church?

....

....

....

What sort of revelation can they bring to the nation?

....

....

....

How, practically, can you encourage and support the ministry of prophets?

....

....

....

judging revelation

Which prophetic revelations carry the same level of inspiration as Scripture?

....

....

Which prophetic revelations should not be judged?

....

....

What does 1 Corinthians 14:30 teach about the inspiration and importance of prophecy?

....

....

....

What are the three principle purposes of God's Word?

....

....

....

How should we judge prophecies which do not seem to share any of these purposes?

....

....

At the moment, how is prophecy judged in your church?

....

....

....

....

At the moment, how do you judge personal revelations?

....

....

....

JUDGING REVELATION

Suggest a revelation which would fail the functional tests on page 108.

....

....

Suggest a revelation which would pass the functional tests.

....

....

Suggest a revelation which would fail the theological tests on page 108.

....

....

Suggest a revelation which would pass the theological tests.

....

....

Suggest a revelation which would fail the moral tests on page 109.

....

....

Suggest a revelation which would pass the moral tests.

....

....

Who should be involved in judging prophecy?

....

....

What needs to change for your church to judge prophecy more thoroughly, and in a more biblical manner?

....

....

....

....

TESTING PERSONAL PROPHECY

How can we identify a false prophet?

....

....

....

Suggest a few personal revelations which would fail the tests on Pages 112–114.

....

....

....

....

Suggest a few personal revelations which would pass the tests on Pages 112–114.

....

....

....

....

In the past, what personal revelation have you rejected – and why did you do this?

....

....

....

....

Which revelation have you accepted that you now think you should have rejected – and which have you rejected that you now think you should have accepted?

....

....

....

....

....

DEVELOPING PROPHETIC LISTENING

Why is the devil firmly opposed to prophecy?

....

....

....

....

What is the great value of prophecy?

....

....

....

....

If you are a leader, what – specifically – is God now calling you to do to develop prophetic listening in your church? ....

....

....

....

....

....

....

If you are a member, what – specifically – is God now calling you to do to help your leaders develop prophetic listening in your church?

....

....

....

....

....

....

To which parts of the Bible do you need to pay more attention? Why is this?

....

....

What changes is God asking you to make in the way you handle the Scriptures?

....

....

....

....

What are your greatest fears about listening to God and speaking his Word to others?

....

....

....

....

How should you overcome these fears?

....

....

....

What practical changes is God asking you to make in the way that you listen to him?

....

....

....

....

....

....

....

....

....

....